RESEARCH INTO TEACHING METHODS IN HIGHER EDUCATION

MAINLY IN BRITISH UNIVERSITIES

Fourth edition

by

Ruth M. Beard MSc MA PhD

Donald A. Bligh BA PhD

and

Alan G. Harding MA PhD AIM Al Ceram

Society for Research into Higher Education Ltd

NOTES ON AUTHORS

Dr Ruth Beard is the holder of two degrees in mathematics and two in education. She has taught in secondary schools, a college of education, and three universities. Between 1965 and 1973 she was Senior Lecturer in charge of the University Teaching Methods Unit of the University of London Institute of Education. She became Professor of Educational Studies at the University of Bradford in 1973.

Dr Donald Bligh, after studying at a teachers' training college, took degrees in geography, philosophy, and psychology. He has taught in universities, a polytechnic, art and technical colleges, and in non-vocational adult education. He has conducted courses for university teachers in Asia, Africa, Europe, and North America under the aegis of bodies such as UNESCO, the Inter-University Council, the British Council, and WHO. While at London's University Teaching Methods Unit he became known for his books and broadcasts on higher education. He is now Director of Teaching Services at the University of Exeter.

Dr Alan Harding qualified initially as a metallurgist. After five years in industry and a further five years as a research metallurgist with the Atomic Energy Authority at Harwell he took up a teaching post at the College of Technology, Bristol. While in his subsequent post as Lecturer in Materials Science at the University of Bath he centred his interests on teaching methods, particularly project work in science and engineering, and read for a MA (Ed) degree at the University of Exeter. From 1971 to 1974 he held the post of Principal Lecturer in Education at Sheffield Polytechnic where he was responsible for teaching methods training courses. While at Sheffield he initiated informal meetings of staff in polytechnics involved in staff training and development, resulting in the setting-up of the Standing Conference on Educational Development Services in Polytechnics. He is currently a Senior Lecturer at the University of Bradford. His recent publications are in the area of philosophy and practice of professional development.

First published September 1967
Second edition September 1968
Third edition July 1971
Fourth edition April 1978

Cover design by Jennie Webb

CONTENTS

CONTENTS (Continued)

<u>development</u> **by** Alan Harding and Harriet Greenaway, and <u>Professional</u>
<u>development</u> **in** higher education: philosophy and practice by Alan Harding
and Susan Sayer, are in preparation.

Ruth M. Beard

PREFACE

The first edition of this monograph which appeared in September 1967, sold out in eight months. Because there were already sixty additional reference which justified one new section and several substantial amplifications of existing sections, it was followed by a second edition, rather than a reprint in September 1968.

This too sold quickly. I therefore decided to prepare a third edition with the aid of my colleague Donald Bligh at the University Teaching Methods Unit, University of London Institute of Education. It appeared, much enlarged, in 1971. Because demand continued we promised to prepare a fourth edition in 1973/4, but it has taken much longer than expected owing to pressure of work in our new posts at Bradford and Exeter.

During the six-year interval from 1971 to 1977 reorganization of the College of Education, involving introduction of new courses and validation of many of them by CNAA, or by universities, has done much to promote interest in course design and in efficiency of courses and teaching methods.

An area of maximum activity has occurred in applying some elements of educational technology to course design, mainly in polytechnics and colleges of education. This involves specifying aims of courses and relating methods in teaching and assessment to them. In most instances, this in no way equate with the detailed analysis of objectives (or specification of steps in learning) which is required in preparing a programmed text and some other courses similarly designed in a systematic way for individual study. Alan Harding ha joined the authors to write a section on aims and objectives. Various kinds of systematically designed courses, mostly based on the ideas of Postlethwait (1964) and Keller (1968) in America, are dealt with in Chapter 6 under the heading Assessment of Courses, since one of their features is that progress in each successive task is assessed continuously.

Other sections of notable growth, which have also been rewritten, include: use of computers to assist teaching, programmed learning, teaching by television, study methods, oral skills and group discussion, simulation and games.

References have been dropped for a number of reasons. Some have been su seded by new findings or by more thorough and extensive investigations. If they may feature as one item in a survey. Others are omitted for the sake brevity; these apply only to specialized fields, or are concerned with selec of students which seems not strictly relevant to the subject of the text. In addition, reference to Courses and Services for Teachers in Higher Educat no longer appear here because this area has grown sufficiently to justify separate publication in two monographs: <u>The growth of policies in staff</u>

INTRODUCTION

The last ten years have seen considerable increase of both interest in, and contributions to, educational research by teachers in higher education. This activity was in part initiated by formation of the Society for Research into Higher Education in 1964. The Society's Abstracts and Register of Research enabled research workers in the field to contact each other more readily and to keep abreast of developments.

Introduction of journals concerned with research and development in teaching methods in higher education began a little earlier, with the International Journal of Electrical Engineering Education in 1963 and the Bulletin of Mechanical Engineering Education in 1962. The Association for the Study of Medical Education which was set up in the early 60s began publication of the British Journal of Medical Education in 1966. The Centre for Information on Language Teaching kept a register of current research from its inception in 1966. Only seven years later this included more than one hundred references to research into the teaching and learning of students and adults (Lunt, 1973). In the latter half of the decade, physicists, chemists, biologists, and mathematicians commenced publication of journals containing articles on research and developments in teaching, course design and assessment.

The Society for Research into Higher Education served mainly universities, polytechnics, and a small but growing membership from colleges of education, whilst the National Foundation of Educational Research provided services for teachers, publishing many books and papers related to research on teacher education. More recently, The British Educational Research Association, formed in 1973, has brough together research workers from all areas of educational studies including philosophers, historians, psychologists, sociologists, economists, administrators, and statisticians. This should promote interdisciplinary discussion, so leading to improvement in the quality of educational research and to growth of interdisciplinary investigations.

In discussing the growing involvement of teachers in educational research (which is not confined to teachers in higher education), a sociologist suggests that transition to a rapidly changing society forces teachers to play a more dynamic and self-conscious role, re-examining the content and underlying assumptions of the curriculum at all levels. He suggests, further, that we need to generate a new model of teacher education and educational practice, the basic aim being to produce self-critical researching teachers who will constantly monitor the effects of their own and their colleagues' activities, modifying their behaviour accordingly. Teaching itself should become a self-critical research act, and educational research, far from being the remote preserve of a few specialists, should be part of the normal activity in schools and colleges (Gorbutt, 1974).

Although this change is certainly under way in higher education, there are many university teachers still unaffected by it. In some cases they are simply unaware of the changes that are in progress. To some of these teachers, students' failure is simply a consequence of their being poor students, or of schools failing to prepare them adequately. It is not perceived as in part a consequence of teaching which does not meet students' needs or of failure to mark work informatively.

A quite different cause of avoidance of educational research is that some scientists whose subjects have a sound theoretical foundation do not feel at home with a subject which lacks a theory. For not only is there no theory of teaching to turn to when problems arise, but theories of learning are too numerous and too little concerned with academic learning to provide a frame-work for action. Teachers cannot design courses taking into account the numerous variables in learning and personal interactions, but must introduce innovations largely on the basis of induction from their observations. Nevertheless, we should expect that scientists, if not other university teachers, would appreciate the need for experiment to determine the effective-ness of innovations introduced in teaching.

On the whole such an attitude has been less prevalent among biologists, doctors, dentists, psychologists, and specialists in education, all of whom are accustomed to experimenting with variable, living organisms, than among mathematicians, physicists, chemists, and engineers, who handle or observe more predictable inanimate materials and symbols. What differences there are probably arise from basic differences in experience; some physical scientists consider experiments non-scientific if the conclusions can be stated only in terms of probabilities. Since, in addition, by no means all edu-cational experiments are rigorously designed, some tend to reject the results altogether. But, in doing so, they discard the few sound beginnings in scientific method which have so far been made in the educational field and revert to attitudes and subjective judgements appropriate to a pre-scientific era. The remedies lie in more widespread use of good designs in educational experiments as well as appreciation on the part of teachers that results of experiments which are stated only in terms of probabilities may yet have value in guiding policies or in the selection of teaching methods.

Until comparatively recently all changes in university teaching were due to outstanding innovators in the universities, or followed on recommendations of committees and professional bodies. Few of these have been directly influenced by findings in the psychology of learning or experiments into the effectiveness of teaching methods; they were based almost exclusively on teachers' views as to how the subject should develop, their experience of learning and teaching and knowledge of methods used elsewhere. The findings of psychologists are unlikely to supersede such recommendations by experts but should contribute to them increasingly. For example, in the case of preparing programmed books, or setting up television as an aid to teaching, expenditure of time or money may be considerable. Consequently there has been a fairly large number of experiments to determine their value compared with traditional teaching. It is also the psychologists, and lecturers who have taken part in teaching experiments, who have made us aware that some innovations in teaching prove to be stimulating for a time, like fashions, but may soon produce no more response than their predecessors. Consequently any conscientious attempt to devise ways of teaching which are essentially more effective must involve the teacher in specifying his aims, devising methods to achieve them, and undertaking, or allowing, an evaluation of their success in terms of students' achievements and attitudes over a period of time.

The experimental work mentioned in the ensuing pages is mostly restricted to British sources up to early 1976. American work is more extensive (see Eckert and Neale, 1965; McKeachie, 1966; Trent and Cohen, 1973) but this will be referred to only where it is more pertinent than any British source.

CHAPTER 1:   AIMS AND OBJECTIVES

I: NATURE OF AIMS AND OBJECTIVES

Education in the formal, institutional sense requires 'intent' on the part of society, educational institutions, teachers and students. Intentions may be looked at in a number of ways:

a.   Purpose for the educational experience

Although there are internal differences in the attitudes of any interest group, and among the viewpoints of students, teachers, administration, and government (Tropp, 1969), some common points of focus are:

    (i)   to provide opportunities for the intellectual and social development of each individual;

    (ii) to contribute to national development in terms of professional competence and social and economic values; and

    (iii) to extend knowledge and develop a stockpile of expertise while passing on knowledge and characteristics of the culture.

b.   Desired characteristics of educational output

These may range from general to specific competencies and include the familiar areas of attitudes, knowledge and skills.

c.   Selected process and content

This involves the experiences and teaching methods a student will encounter, and the specific course, subject matter and syllabus with which the student is expected to deal.

It is sometimes forgotten that 'aims and objectives' may refer to different aspects of intention on different occasions; but the three aspects of intention listed above are, broadly speaking, what we mean when we use the term. They are discussed more fully below.

d.   Purpose

It is difficult to determine the extent to which the recent focus on defining aims and objectives has had an effect on the practice and effectiveness of education. Demands have been made for more effective and systematic approaches to teaching and learning, and for changes in teaching methods (University Grants Committee 1964, 1965). But the last two decades have also witnessed major social, economic and technical developments which themselves have affected the aims and objectives of higher education.

The period 1956-1970 saw the establishment of many new institutions. Intended both to keep pace with the growth in demand for higher education and to offer alternative resources through up-dated philosophies, polytechnics, 'new' universities and technological universities sought, by developing their new aims, to establish a distinct identity while confirming their comparability in terms of academic status (Crossland 1967). There were calls for 'relevance' and for correspondence to the needs of society (Ministry of Education 1956); calls for greater choice in study options; and movements in the level of support for courses as student interests fluctuated. Robbins (Committee on Higher Education, 1963) recommended that a greater proportion of under-graduates should receive a broader education and that whenever possible the decision between general or special courses should be deferred to the end of the first year. Both the Swann (1968) and McCarthy (1968) reports concluded that only 40 per cent of scientists would be required to have highly specialised knowledge and recommended that the majority of students should take a two-year course in science to provide a knowledge of basic principles. Under-lying both these potential and realised changes was the dramatic growth in student numbers and a matching dynamic within institutions due to the collec-tive aspirations of individual members of staff (Ollerenshaw 1972).

e. Output

In considering research into the general aims of education and the specific objectives of courses, one is faced with a dynamic situation comprising so many variables that modelling, or even simple description, is very difficult. In a factorial study in Australia (Katz and Katz, 1968), three clusters of objectives were identified by students: the first emphasising general and liberalising effects desired from a university education, the second concerned with development of expertise in a special field, and the third with training for a specific vocation.

In a study of the purpose and structure of higher education, Entwistle, Percy and Nisbet (1971) sought to analyse the many diffuse viewpoints in order to construct a logical framework of concepts within which agreement on the objectives of higher education could be sought. Through a literature review and analysis of the stated aims and subsequent actions of institutions, they concluded that "writers in British universities subscribe to a myth — they believe in the existence of the 'idea of the university' but, while the idea inspires respect, pride and affection, there is no stable, readily agreed-upon idea with clear implications for practice". Comparing universities, polytechnics, and colleges of education they found no simple connection between declared institutional objectives and what happened within these institutions. In fact they noted that the status disparity between institutions, the resultant 'academic process' of low status institutions towards degree work, and increased dependence on government finance, were key factors in shaping the daily aims and actions of an institution.

f. Process and Content

Another factor which has contributed a great deal to the demand for clearer aims and objectives is the move towards interdisciplinary courses and modular programmes (Group for Research and Innovation in Higher Education, 1976). Since academics responsible for developing such courses were generally educated in a single discipline, they found it difficult to modify aims, to understand what other specialists were talking about, to sacrifice valued areas of their original discipline or to seek connection and inter-relatedness with associated or contrasting studies.

Interdisciplinarity appears in many forms (Group for Research into Higher Education, 1974a, 1975). A study of the prospectuses for universities and polytechnics reveals considerable variety. Universities such as Sussex and Lancaster have sought to introduce options, some of which complement the major subject, others which contrast with the central theme. Keele has a foundation year which emphasises the scope, methods and inter-connectedness of many branches of university studies.

Elkins (1974) identified four general clusters in interdisciplinary studies:

1. Social Sciences;
2. Cultural and Cognitive Studies;
3. Science, Technology and Society;
4. Design of Human Environments.

In general there are two ways of broadening professional degrees, one reflecting the aims of a liberal education and the other stressing development of social responsibility (Group for Research into Higher Education, 1974b). But in many cases, the aims of interdisciplinary studies become complex and difficult to evaluate. Piaget (1972) attempted to alleviate some of the existing confusion by devising an epistomology of interdisciplinary relationships. He sought to differentiate between multidisciplinary, interdisciplinary and trans-disciplinary programmes in terms of the degree of interaction between their components. With a clearer framework it may be possible in future to examine how so-called interdisciplinary courses are meeting their aims.

One further major development in the broadening of aims and related practices in higher education should also be included: the move towards problem-oriented and project-oriented studies. In such courses the authority role of staff is moderated as they begin to function more as 'facilitators', guides and providers of resources (Adderley et al, 1975). In a problem-oriented course leading to a graduate certificate in education, the students construct their own course programme on the basis of their own needs and interests, having an opportunity to propose, formulate and select course objectives (Chadwick, 1974). At Lancaster, a system of Independent Studies allows students to spend most of the last four terms on a single project of their own choosing (Wilby, 1976). In various European countries the aims and processes of project-oriented studies have been deemed of such major importance that a number of

their universities have been wholly or largely devoted to a project approach
(University of Bremen, 1976).

II: SPECIFICATION OF AIMS AND OBJECTIVES

a. The Behavioural Approach

Proponents of a comprehensive and systematic approach to teaching and
learning (Eraut, 1970) argue that in any learning process it is necessary to
first describe, in behavioural terms, what students will be able to do at the
end of a course (Bloom, 1954; Mager, 1971). Five logical reasons are
advanced for specifying objectives at the outset (Bligh et al. 1975).

Unless we know what we want the students to achieve:

(i)   we cannot assess whether they have achieved it;

(ii)   we cannot select students most likely to achieve it;

(iii)   we cannot decide what content to teach so that they achieve it;

(iv)   we cannot choose the best methods to use in order to achieve it;

(v)   we will be limited in testing the effectiveness of our own teaching.

Other reasons given are that the analysis of objectives can reveal hidden
assumptions in one's teaching and omissions in coverage; that the statement
of objectives makes it easier for students to monitor their progress towards
a goal; and that clear objectives focus the teacher's attention on results and
on the student's attainments rather than on his/her own role.

Many opinions and studies support such views. The Postlethwait (1964) and
Keller (1968) Plans have been followed with success in the United States,
Canada, Australia, and the United Kingdom. Improvement in examination
performance and better retention of anatomical knowledge was observed by
giving 'proper' attention to clear objectives, and allowing active participation
of students and prompt feedback (Blizard and Blunt, 1975). Students given
behavioural objectives in anatomy were found to have a better score on recall
and problem-solving, and greater retention, than students who were not made
aware of the objectives (Varaguman, 1971). Baume and Jones (1974) have
achieved positive results in engineering courses and have recommended
specific procedures for starting with general aims and systematically making
them more precise.

But although the behavioural objectives approach is intrinsically logical and
attractive, it is not universally acclaimed. Its tendency towards prescription
of ways in which student success may be promoted and evaluated are seen by
some as untenable. They ask, for example, who determines the objectives,
and why those particular objectives are chosen (Rowntree, 1973). The idea
of logically prescribing a learning system is also questioned, since learners

favour different paths (Pask and Scott, 1971; Lewis, 1974). It is suggested
that there may be two fundamental errors in a behavioural approach:

(i)   that subject matter, knowledge, and skills cannot be adequately
      represented by a list of items since it is the inter-connectedness
      of knowledge that matters most;

(ii) that concepts cannot be adequately represented by a list of
      behaviours since advanced learning depends upon valuing and
      being willing to recognise hypotheses as the growth points of
      personal knowledge (McDonald Ross, 1972).

At the Advisory Centre for University Education at Adelaide, an attempt is
being made to avoid what are seen as 'errors' inherent in a classical linear
model of curriculum development through the use of a more open model (Hall,
1975). As a result of experience with the Inter-University Biology Project,
Dowdeswell (1972) suggested that an interactive model was more appropriate
since formal statements of objectives in operational terms were usually not
possible until the development of relevant materials was at least partly
completed. Further arguments against seeking to describe objectives in rigid
behavioural terms are that the task is time-consuming, that the results are
frequently inadequate, that there is little consistent or repeatable evidence to
show that it produces a substantial improvement in the quality of graduates or
in the effectiveness of learning. These latter points are extremely difficult to
assess due to the progressive nature of educational developments and the
dynamic interaction of education and society (Parlett and Hamilton, 1972).

Adding to such objections, Woolfenden (1969) suggested on a more practical
level that the widespread use of objectives in medical education is prevented
by a number of factors: there is no agreed set of objectives; the system
works now, so why change?; there is not enough evidence of what a doctor is
required to do; there is a problem of uncertainty in terms of cause and effect;
interpersonal skills are difficult to specify; and a set of specified objectives
would not, in any case, be a prescription for successful teaching.

In teaching law, however, similar objections were made to development of
postgraduate courses specifying objectives and relating these with planned
activities, materials or equipment, and method of evaluation; but Ross (1972-6)
has developed courses of this kind. Before he did so, some colleagues
considered the task impossible; afterwards they described his method as
'obvious'.

b.   Interpretation of Aims

Perhaps in an avoidance of some of the problems imputed to an extreme
behavioural approach, many people tend to concentrate on what are referred
to as 'intermediate' goals — factors that constitute professional competence
in a given field, appropriate professional attitudes and requisite intellectual
skills. Such intermediate aims are believed to be of great importance in

giving direction to learning and in promoting confidence and motivation by their specific achievement. Beard, Healey, and Holloway (1969) examined the relationship between such objectives and the nature of the teaching process. Comprehensive analysis of intermediate objectives in an Art College (Burke, 1967; Piper, 1967) led to the complete re-organisation of a course for designers by discarding the traditional subject-based course in favour of a project-oriented approach.

Sample intermediate aims and their accompanying objectives are provided by E.A.H. Martin (Department of Botany, Glasgow University, unpublished):

"A.   Aim: 'To understand the Hardy-Weinberg Law'

Objectives: 1.   The student will be able to give a written definition of the law.

2.   The student will be able to derive the Hardy-Weinberg formula.

3.   The student will be able to list four conditions described in a population before the gene frequencies given by the formula will be valid.

B.   Aim: 'To understand sex-linked inheritance'

Objectives: 1.   Given several family trees, the student will be able to select those in which there is a sex-linked trait.

2.   The student will be able to forecast the percentage of affected individuals of a mating, given the genotype of the parents."

A similar example from an electrical engineering course is provided by J.B. Thomas (Brunel University, unpublished):

"Aim: 'To understand magnetohydrodynamic power generation (MHD)'

Objectives: 1.   To give a brief but accurate account, in descriptive terms of the basic physical principles of MHD generation.

2.   To draw a sketch which illustrates unambiguously the reasons for the MHD power generation, in terms of the movement of hot ionised gases through a magnetic field, etc.

3.   To list the practical problems arising from the high temperature required for MHD generation.

4.   To list, compare and contrast, the advantages and disadvantages of the open and closed cycles for MHD generation.

5. To discuss the forecast of the economics of MHD generation in terms of:–

    5.1 capital expenditure and running costs of MHD plant;

    5.2 'topping up' conventional steam plant. "

But such a tidy and informative approach continues to invite criticism. Many established teachers argue that such items as listed in the biology and electrical engineering examples are obvious, traditional, and require no special study or extensive analysis. More importantly, many question whether there is general agreement about the meaning of their common aim — "to understand..."

This query should not be dismissed as mere semantic bickering. In two inquiries into the aims and choices of teaching methods among 21 teachers in a department of psychiatry, Walton and Drewery (1964, 1966) found that every teacher stated as one of his objectives the provision of systematic information. This was the exclusive goal of three of them, six others taught with a psycho-dynamic orientation, seven shared these goals but also aimed to teach behavioural science, while the remaining five aimed, in addition, to modify the behaviour of students. Discussion would undoubtedly show that members of staff had different interpretations of 'systematic information', or that they were likely to disagree about methods of determining whether this objective had been attained.

Differences of interpretation are not limited to terminology but may also involve application of teaching methods. In a pilot inquiry into the use of small group discussion in Departments of Mathematics, Electrical Engineering, and Biology in London University, Beard (1967a) found that lecturers in any one subject had many different aims in using discussion, and also observed some differentiation between subjects.

In searching for objectives in introductory courses in English Law, Power (1972) classified intermediate level examinations in English Law in accordance with Bloom's Taxonomy and discussed his observations with the three examining bodies. He found that examiners were not consistent in the objectives they wished students to achieve and, further, that regardless of the aims stated, in most papers success was possible with no more than memorised information.

At Surrey, Boud (1973) studied differences between the aims expressed by staff and students in connection with laboratory work, and between the 'intended' and 'actual' aims perceived by staff conducting laboratory classes.

Entwistle, Percy, and Nisbet (1971) also examined the differences in objectives and actual teaching. While acknowledging that their conclusions were impressions rather than the results of a substantial study, they found that general teaching objectives are much the same in all institutions of higher education. Staff tended to believe that the sort of person 'produced' mattered more than the absorption of factual information. However, there was also a lack of relation between intention and performance; only a tenuous connection could be found between 'teaching objectives' (what the lecturers say they want to achieve) and the 'teaching activity' (what they actually do).

III : DETERMINATION OF AIMS AND OBJECTIVES

Eggleston (1969) suggested six methods for identifying teaching objectives:

1. reference to the literature;

2. seeking justification for the introduction of new elements in a course, or a revision of existing elements;

3. examination of the demands made on students during the learning process;

4. study of demands made on students in examination or other assessment procedures;

5. through the introduction of new forms of test items;

6. reference to lists of objectives in relevant or related disciplines.

Of the many studies concerning educational aims, relatively few have specified objectives as a basis for direct action in modifying or remediating courses; a larger number have concentrated on trying to identify the actual aims and objectives which are in force in various disciplines. However, in the former category there are some useful examples.

Dudley (1970) made an attempt to translate the general aims of the Royal Commission on Medical Education into explicit educational objectives which would relate to the details of curriculum design. The Royal College of General Practitioners (1969) derived a statement of the crucial elements of being a competent general practitioner for the 70s from a study of existing knowledge, experience and research. Freeman and Byrne (1973) analysed these aims at the departmental level, then expanded and reclassified the departmental objectives into behavioural objectives using the critical incident technique to distinguish between acceptable and unacceptable behaviours. As a prelude to introducing fundamental changes in the education of teachers, the University of Leeds Institute of Education (1973) undertook a major study of the objectives of teacher education.

Attempts to elicit existing objectives are more numerous. Cope (1969) interviewed students, college staff and teachers involved in school practice to obtain a statement of the objectives of school practice. Tutors, students of the colleges, and school teachers in the colleges of education at the Birmingham University Institute of Education, were surveyed to determine the objectives of teaching psychology to student teachers. Beard and Pole (1971) discussed examination papers with internal examiners, to determine their objectives in examining biochemistry in ten colleges of the University of London. At the University of Bath all staff contributing to the engineering courses were invited to specify their course objectives and the information was made available as a student handbook (Black, 1974). Staff in engineering departments at Scottish universities are being interviewed in an attempt to determine and collate objectives in engineering education (Boud 1976).

A number of other studies show slightly different approaches. Through staff surveys, analysis of the literature and study of the teaching process, Harding (1973a) and Cornwall (1975) identified aims and objectives required in professional roles as scientists and engineers which were not normally specified in undergraduate courses. By similar means Harding and Sayer (1975) derived aims and objectives for emerging staff training and professional development programmes in universities.

A number of people have also solicited views and information outside the educational institution. Hopkins (1967) drew up a user classification: a scale of importance for subjects encountered in metallurgy courses. Jones (1969) determined ratings of the professional skills required of physicists and chemists and compared the requirements to actual instruction received. The most systematic study of the relationship between professional needs and objectives in professional education has been made in the field of engineering (Heywood, Youngman, Monk, and Oxtoby, 1973; Heywood, 1975). Training objectives were derived from task-analyses and studies of attitudes and organisational factors in an industrial engineering enterprise.

IV: CONTEXT

Whatever the form or nature of particular specification of aims and objectives, in the long run it is what the teacher does that counts. Admiration for the teaching role and genuine concern for students may count more heavily in the teacher's contribution than any particular set of aims or attitudes thereto (Sayer and Harding, 1974). "Undeclared or unconscious attitudes of staff and of an institution may be a much larger influence, over-riding the influence that the formal syllabuses may be supposed to have in forming students" (Lane, 1974).

CHAPTER 2: ECONOMY AND EFFICIENCY

Under this heading we shall consider experiments in which one important criterion was either cost, or the time spent by students or staff. Efficiency is normally the effectiveness of the teaching methods in terms of student learning in relation to one or more of these factors. The factors may also be combined to produce composite measures such as the cost per student hour or the ratio of staff time to student time.

In the third edition of this volume we observed that economists were beginning to investigate the efficiency and productivity of university eduation (eg Blaug, 1968). The current financial crisis makes such studies more urgent and a few are already published. Layard and Oatey (1973) attempt to assess the cost-effectiveness of each kind of new media in higher education. For example they contrast the costs per student hour of teaching by television with that of live lectures. Since there appears to be little difference in their effectiveness (Chu and Scramm, 1967) they believe mechanical methods of presentation should be encouraged.

Hoos (1975) warns that industrial style 'efficiency' may prove more costly than beneficial in education. It depends on the criterion of 'efficiency'. If the cost of graduates produced is related to staff-student ratios, there could appear to be a case for increasing the size of classes. Pickford (1975) has suggested that the need for university resources should not rise proportionately with student numbers and the larger universities do not make optimal use of resources. A report by Layard and Verry (1975) implies that as departments in the arts and social sciences become larger, research time is sacrificed to teaching. This does not appear to happen amongst physical and biological scientists. Although their figures may now be out of date, they have also calculated that the average postgraduate costs three times as much to educate as the average undergraduate and six times as much in mathematics and the physical sciences. The ratio assumed by the UGC is normally $2:1$. When Laidlaw and Layard (1975) compared the costs of Open University courses with those of traditional universities, with one exception they found the former cheaper. Foundation courses proved much cheaper than the equivalent provision de novo in campus universities.

Only two experiments described in British journals are specifically concerned with class size: de Cecco (1964) assigned 682 students randomly to three kinds of groups, two large experimental ones consisting of 97 and 127 subjects, six small experimental groups ranging in size from 18 to 34 subjects and 10 small control groups ranging from 22 to 35. All courses in the experimental groups followed the same outline including major assignments, instructional materials and a common grading system but, in the control group, instructors proceeded as normal, selecting their own materials and creating their own assignments. In the four tests given subsequently, no significant differences were found in acquisition of information or understanding but the students greatly preferred smaller groups.

Cottrell (1962) used groups of 3, 12 and 24 members in an attempt to discover how large a discussion group could be in physical chemistry without loss of efficiency. A short answer-paper was set on matters of fact and simple problems following weekly discussions throughout one term. Groups as large as 24 proved unpopular and inefficient. The success ratio (calculated by dividing each student's score by his mean marks in class examinations in chemistry the previous year) was consistently higher for the groups of 12.

Extensive studies on the class size made in the United States, having conflicting results, are reported by McKeachie (1966) who concludes that the importance of size depends on educational goals: "In general, large classes are simply not as effective as small classes for retention, critical thinking and attitude change".

Yet surveying a similar literature, Bligh (1972a) came to a different conclusion in the case of lectures. Although the majority of experiments show no significant difference in the effectiveness of large and small classes, the direction of the small differences obtained usually favours larger classes. The popular opinion among teachers and students is the reverse when asked directly, but not when indirect evidence on students' attitudes is obtained. Possibly public discussion about class sizes in schools has established a 'right' answer in their minds. The students' role in lectures is not greatly changed by increases in class size, but skills required by the lecturers are.

However, a recent finding by Wood, Linsky, and Strauss (1975) shows that students rate small and large classes higher than those of the 'medium' size of 250. The reasons for this have not been explored.

A different approach to study of efficiency has been made in Moscow where students' times of optimal work performance have been studied in relation to demands of the academic time-table (Doskin and Laurent'eva, 1974). The results showed that for a sample of 108 students, periods of maximum physiological alertness and optimal work performance coincided; these occurred between 9 am and 2 pm for 55 percent of the sample (the morning type), between 3 pm and midnight for 35 percent (the evening type), but fluctuated randomly for the remaining 10 percent. They conclude that 'morning type' students are best adapted to the existing teaching arrangements, while 'evening type' students are most disadvantaged; but this seems to assume that alertness is more beneficial in class than in independent study, while Bligh (1974) has shown the reverse to be true.

Experiments in which an important objective is to reduce time occupied in teaching have been conducted with a variety of methods. Tubbs (1968) reports that he works with groups of about eight students to help them to learn more about experimentation. A problem is outlined by the tutor, suggestions are invited from students, and these are discussed in some detail. The students then choose apparatus and spend three or four hours in making measurements, each in a different way. Finally they discuss reasons for differences in their results and sources of experimental error. The method proves economical of staff time and, usually, of apparatus. Tubbs considers that first year students can usefully spend up to twenty percent of laboratory time in this way. However, there is no experimental evaluation of the method.

Programmed learning is another development which offers the tutor an opportunity to reduce instruction time. A series of experiments to compare programmed learning in science using one teacher, with conventional teaching using two, has been made very successfully in the Navy (Stavert and Wingate, 1966). Ten pairs of classes were taught by conventional methods or by programmed learning in basic electronics, basic radio and in associated laboratory work. While one group followed the programme and illustrative films with the aid of a junior technician, the other received conventional teaching from an Instruction Officer. Since in every case results from programmed learning equalled or excelled those of conventional teaching it was clearly possible, and indeed even beneficial, to cut instruction time by half. Failure rates were 14 percent and 3 percent less, and final average marks were 62 in each case as compared with 55 and 54, in electronics and radio respectively. In addition, time taken by programmed learning in radio was 25 percent less, on average, than that for conventional instruction. Experiments in the RAF confirm that, over a period of weeks, students using programmed learning took considerably less time, particularly in the case of those using a programme reduced to essentials, but achieved results similar to those of apprentices studying by conventional methods (Wallis et al, 1966). This has been confirmed in a course for medical science personnel who attempted programmes having five differing amounts of redundancy (Valverdi and Morgan, 1970). The leanest programme proved most economical and efficient. Statistics programmes seem to be less successful, however. J.R. Hartley (1968) reports a study with 138 university students in which a programme exerted greater control over students' work habits and led to a higher overall mean mark on tests of retention, application and transfer; but 47 percent of the students completed less than three-quarters of the programme compared with only 19 percent of the control group who failed to read the book. Thus in this case the programme achieved a better result at the expense of greater effort which was unacceptable to many students; but the possibility of cutting the programme is not discussed.

It may be that findings in the Forces and in industry are irrelevant at university level. Only experiments with carefully prepared programmes can show whether this is so, but experiments in universities also show savings in time. Moore (1967) found in an experiment with university students that group teaching by a method of pacing, setting a time limit for each frame, resulted in a considerably better speed for slow workers. Times for the machine group were of the order of 30 percent less than that of slower workers using self-paced books. This saving was effected without significantly affecting the test scores. Biran and Pickering (1968) found that 'unscrambling' a branching programme in genetics and presenting it in linear form decreased learning time without affecting gain in scores. Teather (1968), in listing programmes for teaching biology, notes the saving in time and the possibility of using programmes for experiments with alternative teaching sequences.

Comparisons of different conventional methods of teaching show that the lecture is more economical of time than other methods if each is used independently. Joyce and Weatherall (1957), in comparing different methods of teaching (lectures, discussion groups, practical classes and unsupervised reading) in a carefully designed experiment, concluded that lecturing was the most efficient method of teaching since it used least of the students' and staff's time: "For tutors the size of classes is relevent to the economics of teaching, and the figures amount to 0.05 hours per session per student for lectures (assuming an audience of 60); 0.3 hours per session per student for discussion groups of 12 students, and 0.33 hours per session per student for practical classes on the same scale... these estimates are probably reliable enough to emphasise the economy, both to students and staff, of lecturing compared with practical classes and discussion groups..." But they commented that a simple comparison of the four methods might not have shown all of them to the best advantage: for example, discussion groups might have been more efficient when used to develop material already presented by other methods.

In a second experiment (1959) they used a more complex but equally carefully chosen design, to compare methods in which the contribution of teachers' time was small with others in which the teachers were more fully involved. Sixty-two clinical students were taught by four initial lectures and either three demonstrations or three practical classes in conjunction with either three conventional seminars or three discussion meetings initiated by playing back recorded material. Gain in knowledge did not differ significantly from one group to another, but demonstrations were much more economical of time than practical classes for teachers, technicians and students (practicals taking about 20 percent more time for students and teachers); discussion required less time of teachers than seminars, but the corresponding difference for students was slight.

MacManaway (1968) confirmed the efficiency of lectures in comparing recall of lecture material and the same material learned by reading lecture scripts and note-taking. Reading and note-taking took considerably longer, but, in a test given a week later, students in both groups did about equally well. A third group who attended the lecture and made notes subsequently took still more time but did no better.

One experiment, however, shows that combination of methods, using some discussion but no lectures, may be highly efficient. To Erskine and Tomkin (1963), reduction of time spent on a course was a major consideration. They substituted two periods of group discussion for nine lectures during a period of three weeks spent in studying the anatomy of the pelvis. Following an introductory demonstration using specially prepared specimens and models, practical work was done in the usual way, but with access to practical materials at any time during the day and with informal demonstrations on request. The discussion groups were introduced at the ends of the second and third weeks. On each occasion lists were displayed which drew attention to a number of points in the course of practical work, and a central theme was agreed on for discussion between the four instructors in order to organise the facts into a pattern. Consequently the students arrived well prepared at the discussions, in which there was a free exchange of views resulting in synthesis at the end of each section.

The experiment was not a controlled one in which parallel groups were treated differently, but an attempt was made to assess its success by comparing results of students in two successive years, and each group of students with themselves in anatomy of the pelvis and of the thorax. Objective tests, essays and oral examinations were all used in the assessment. It appeared reasonably clear that there was no loss of information as a result of the change in method, but rather the contrary, and students who attended discussion groups were far more successful in oral examinations. But the chief gain was of seven hours time in the case of each student and one hour to each member of staff.

In this last experiment we have evidence not only of reduction in time spent but also of better recall of recently learned material. Experiments with programmed learning have also resulted in gains in both these respects, but at present there are few programmes suited to university work. However, where recall, or retention, is as good as that for lectures or other methods depending on the presence of teachers, the gain in teaching time is obvious.

Similar gains may be made with more relevant or better planned activities using audio-visual techniques. In an Australian 'experiment' (Collard et al, 1969) in teaching chemistry, university students who constructed organic molecules in plastic and sketched completed models, instead of merely studying from text-books and copying diagrams, showed a marked improvement in understanding of three-dimensional aspects of molecular structure. And in medical teaching in Glasgow, where the ratio of staff to students is low, a collection of programmed tape-slide presentations enables students to work independently at their own speed (Harden et al, 1969); the experimental group using this technique did significantly better than the control group who followed a conventional course, the three overseas students rising from the lower to the upper half of the class as a whole. Lewinson (1970) reports self-testing devices in clinical medicine using a quiz board displaying pictures, slides or X-rays together with questions as to diagnosis etc. A lift-up card displays answers and a folder supplies references. The advantage of the method is that it can be used during spare intervals and a third of the students say that they find it valuable.

Since the last publication of this book the use of computers to assist teaching in higher education has greatly increased. For example at Napier College the feasibility of using computers to teach mathematics to engineering and business studies students is being investigated. Using the techniques of branching programmes (see page 30) attempts have been made to provide instruction and correction of errors according to the needs of each individual; but the time spent in preparation and the cost of computer space makes this a doubtful investment when the advantages over other methods are marginal. At the New University of Ulster the computer is used as a 'manager of learning' by marking tests and prescribing routes for individual students through a series of course modules (Hooper, 1974).

If computers are used to perform complex mathematical calculations, students may gain the satisfaction of acquiring and testing new concepts without the frustration and delay normally experienced through necessary computation. At the University of Surrey, Cox et al (1974) programmed three types of computer with material in quantum mechanics based upon a Keller course. All three methods appeared satisfactory according to students' evaluations. Computers are used in a similar way at Exeter to test the viability of electrical circuits which cannot be checked directly. Particularly in engineering there is growing cooperation between institutions in higher education in the design and testing of computerised learning packages.

There is no compelling evidence at the present time that computer assisted instruction (CAI) results in better learning than other methods. Its merit lies in savings of time and effort. Computers can be used to present information, but they are no more effective at doing this than a programmed text, tape-recorder, television set, or book. When the initial outlay in time, effort and money is greater than with conventional teaching, new methods with marginal benefit are best used on courses unlikely to change from year to year. It is for this reason, as well as the fact that computers are most useful when dealing with numbers rather than words and that staff are accustomed to using them, that CAI has been most popular in physical, mathematical and engineering sciences.

At the University of Kent the use of computers to search legal texts is being developed to help students search complete documents such as statutes, treaties, and law reports (Niblett, 1976). Exeter University Teaching Services is developing a computerised system by which abstracts of research and experiments in higher education, or parts of abstracts such as the experimental aims or methods, may be printed in response to appropriate key-words. For example a summary of the literature on multiple-choice questions in medicine included in the system may be obtained by using the key-words 'multiple-choice' and 'medicine'. The National Foundation for Educational Research has a similar system for current research in higher education in conjunction with The Council of Europe.

Activities and information designed to enable students to make better use of
facilities or to benefit from a course also add to efficiency. A one-week,
pre-college mathematics workshop organised by Taylor and Hanson (1969)
led to significantly higher grades for those who attended than for controls who
were initially rated more able, and their attrition rate was considerably lower.
A study by Gardiner, Boddy, and Taylor (1969) shows that in teaching applied
pharmacology, anaesthesiology and hospital procedure, practical experience
in the wards may with advantage be substituted for lectures. Among 74 senior
dental students, the group which spent two days in normal surgical wards —
where teaching was minimal, but practical experience and contact with all
grades of hospital staff were at a maximum — required less time and found it
easier to assimilate information than did the group which attended 22 lectures
during a period of ten weeks (Stuebner and Johnson, 1969). Sandwich courses
have been designed with these advantages in mind but few have been evaluated.
In Canada, at Waterloo (Holmes, 1970) students of engineering who spend
alternate terms in college and in industry are said to have an awareness of,
and confidence in, the opportunities within Canadian industry which has led to
a reduction in the brain drain to the United States. However, satisfaction with
sandwich courses in engineering seems to be limited to some schools and
some courses. Theoretical courses are often overloaded and about half the
students in one inquiry found industrial training unsatisfactory (Heward et al,
1968). Some similar findings have been obtained by Smithers at the University
of Bradford (1976). In further education Jones and Wylie (1976) have concluded
that a scheme of directed private study would be cheaper than either part-time
day release, evening classes, or any other system of training.

Detailed studies of the uses of students' time over a period of a day, or more
probably a week, give a useful indication of the pressure or slackness of work,
attendance at voluntary courses or other activities, etc, and so provide a
basis for changes in the curriculum or, possibly, in teaching methods. In an
early study of this kind Thoday (1957) asked each of over 500 students in
Birmingham University to account in detail for his or her activities on the
previous day. Information was also obtained about main activities during the
previous weekend and a proportion of students were interviewed twice to give
some idea of day-to-day variations. She found that mean time spent in work
per day was six-and-a-quarter hours: three-and-a-half hours in timetable
work and the remaining two-and-three-quarter hours in 'informal work'.
Contrary to belief, female and science students worked no harder than male
or arts students, but the latter did more informal and less set work. Second
year students worked least hard except those studying medicine and modern
languages who had important examinations then. In most subjects students did
more work in the first than in the final year. In an investigation among sixth
formers, students at a college of education and those at a technical university,
Child (1970) found no difference in their study habits except that sixth formers
worked more at week-ends.

Recent studies are far more detailed. Most agree with Entwistle et al (1971)
that, on the average, students work a 36-39 hour week partly in class and

partly in private study. Students resident in a tower block in the University of Essex averaged only 33 hours (Clossick, 1968) and an enquiry by the NUS (Saunders et al, 1969) including further education reported an average of 42 hours per week. There are, of course, wide individual and subject differences. The average number of hours spent in class according to Entwistle's survey was 14 in universities, 19 in colleges of education and 22 in polytechnics. These figures partly reflect the subjects taught. Engineers and physical scientists with large amounts of laboratory work averaged 20 hours. In arts and social sciences class time decreased from 15 hours in the first year to about 6 in the third. The NUS study suggests that students of art and architecture spend about 30 hours in class owing to the amount of studio work.

Where class time is high, private study time is correspondingly reduced. Except for the study by Cooper and Foy (1969) most enquiries have found a positive correlation between time spent and subsequent examination success (see summaries by Miller, 1970; Bligh et al, 1975).

Of considerable importance when planning and teaching courses are teachers' expectations of student performance both in the time spent and in study efficiency. Available evidence suggests that teachers usually expect too much. In one medical school students were asked to account for time, hourly during the night and quarter-hourly during the day, and to fill in their schedule using code numbers for different activities during one week. Mean times were compared with estimates provided in advance by teachers (Anderson et al, 1968). Clinical students proved to be working 40-50 hours per week but preferred to take more leisure throughout the week and to work during part of the weekend; the first years averaged seven hours per day, while second years averaged six hours. Teachers' estimates corresponded fairly well with average times given to different activities by students except that they supposed students talked shop more than they claimed to do and that they spent far less time in leisure activities than they did. The authors concluded that the failure of students to work hard suggested the course could be more challenging.

In an unpublished study in another clinical department a similar questionnaire was completed and a sample of students was also observed throughout a period of three weeks. Staff supposed that the first year students would spend some seven to eight hours per day in the wards or in study, but their mean time in the hospital proved to be 4.6 hours daily including lunch-hour, with little evidence of additional work. In the observer's opinion the students felt insufficiently involved, at least during this period, to work hard in their course.

This chapter uses relatively few criteria of economy and efficiency. Many others could be developed. For example, an interesting attempt to measure productivity in a university has been made by an economist in Canada (Huber, 1974) who has attempted to predict graduate students' grades in economics on the basis of certain student characteristics — including average grades in the previous year — and on the basis of current-year and past-year instructor effects. Current financial circumstances should allow exploration for similar new measures.

CHAPTER 3: RECALL AND RETENTION OF INFORMATION

I: EXPERIMENTS BASED ON THE FINDINGS OF PSYCHOLOGISTS

Methods of improving immediate recall, or retention, of subject matter are based on what is known of remembering and forgetting in learning. It is known that to assist memory, subject matter should be meaningful, inter-relationships between topics should be stressed, and frequent short periods should be spent in study in preference to a few long ones. Forgetting, on the other hand, is induced by presenting the learner with many unrelated details, or by inter-ference where a new topic is introduced at the end of a period of study or if two closely similar topics are learned together. To encourage accurate recall, correct responses should be rewarded or reinforced immediately (possibly only by knowing that the response is right) while wrong responses should be corrected at once. It is commonly said that errors should be avoided as far as possible. Above all, it is important that the student should make a response, though it may be a purely mental one; to be efficient, his learning must actively employ his ability to organise new information into his existing mental schemes. Where learning takes place by rote, with little understanding, subsequent forget-ting is rapid. Obviously interest is also important; a student who is interested is more likely to play an active part in learning.

Studies in which principles are stressed while details are reduced in number take account of these findings. Erskine and O'Morchoe compared recall follow-ing a course in anatomy in which principles were stressed and details omitted with one of the same length in which details were included (Erskine and O'Morchoe, 1961). But although results appear to be consistent with findings in the psychology of learning, the experiment was performed with groups which were not strictly comparable, since they were in different years and were, presumably, taught by different teachers.

Adams, Daniel, Herxheimer, and Weatherall (1960) made a controlled study into the value of emphasis in the elimination of errors, collecting common errors, testing them on a group of 53 students, and dividing them for the pur-poses of the experiment into matched groups. For the next few months in the experimental group each misconception was deliberately discredited whenever it was relevant to mention it, while misconceptions in the control group received no special attention. At the end of the course, incidence of misconcep-tions of the experimental (emphasised) items had decreased by a highly signifi-cant amount as compared with incidence of misconceptions in control items. Thus there was no support for the common belief among teachers that emphasising errors leads to their perpetuation.

An unexpected finding in this experiment was that the students who attended best had the highest incidence of misconceptions initially. The best attenders showed substantial improvement during the course both on treated and untreated items; moderate attenders improved only on treated items, and the poor attenders showed little improvement, what little there was being mainly in the treated items. Broadly, this provides evidence that the first group of students were probably the most intelligent, who were sensitive even to slight emphases. The writers consider it to be of special interest that this group of students "entered the experiment with the highest incidence of misconceptions and finished with the lowest — that is, the best learners went through a phase of putting forward the selected misconceptions unusually readily". They suggest that this points to a trial and error mechanism of learning, lending support to the saying 'If you don't make mistakes you won't make anything'.

Some light is cast on the seeming contradiction in this experiment (to the belief that it is unwise to emphasise errors) from the results of an experiment by Elley (1966) who contrasted the effect of errors in rote and logical tasks. He used multiple-choice questions allowing different rates of error in the course of learning each task. In rote learning, frequent errors resulted in inaccurate recall, but in logical tasks the rate of error made no difference, for, in these cases, students did not tend to repeat errors which they happened to have made while learning. Elley comments that, in preparing programmed texts for students on meaningful learning tasks, there is no need to be restricted by the assumption that errors must be kept to a minimum due to the interference they occasion in learning. However, in simpler tasks such as acquisition of vocabulary and elementary use of language, methods which lead to error-free learning are the most effective.

Avoidance of interference due to the order of presentation of learning tasks was studied by Leith and McHugh (1967). The questions they wished to answer were whether it was preferable to present a familiar task first, following it with an unfamilar one as is usually advised by teachers, or whether the reverse would result in more effective learning and, in either case, where to introduce a theoretical passage explaining the subject. Students studying anthropology were given three passages: kinship systems of patrilineal and matrilineal tribes and a theoretical passage explaining the significance of kinship and different patterns of marriage, descent and residence. The design of the experiment allowed eight treatments with 80 students; the passages were studied during three 45-minute sessions in one day and a test containing items from all three passages was administered two days later. Analysis of the results showed that students did equally well in questions relating to the familiar, patrilineal system whatever the order of presentation, but they recalled the matrilineal system significantly better if it was presented before the more familiar system, and theory was helpful only if it came between these passages or at the end.

II: FEEDBACK IN LEARNING

The value of feedback has been questioned following an American experiment in which students were given a text to read, a 30 item multiple-choice test, and then one of four conditions: no feedback, immediate feedback, feedback after one day, feedback after one week. No differences in subsequent performance were noted, except that on the basis of questionnaire responses immediate feedback seemed to stimulate more reading (Newman et al, 1974). But prompt and frequent feedback is recommended by other psychologists as an aid to recall and retention of information. The use of continuous feedback (as to the failure or success of learning) is regarded as an essential feature of programmed learning.

Asking questions of students during the lecture period to which they must write the answers, and providing correct answers immediately, proves to be an extremely effective method of teaching (Beard, 1967b). McCarthy (1970) gave feedback to his students by using a step-by-step lecture method in which each of ten or more questions projected on a screen was attempted by the students and discussed by the lecturer before proceeding. The students were supplied with a handout of questions for each lecture to provide a complete record and on which they could write notes. They were generally in favour of the method. It is interesting that the lecturer underestimated the time needed to discuss earlier questions and overestimated students' preknowledge. Thus it seems that feedback to the lecturer during discussion made him slow down to a pace appropriate to the students' ease of understanding.

An adaptable and economical form of feedback to the teacher called the 'Cosford Cube' has been used by Taplin with RAF trainees (1969). Students were each provided with a two-and-a-half inch cube with differently coloured faces which could be held so that a chosen colour visible only to the instructor indicated the answer to a multiple-choice question. Taplin recommends its use both after making critical points and at the end of a lecture; but he found that lectures took longer and required more preparation. Dunn obtained similar results with medical students using coloured cards (1969).

The findings of psychologists that correct responses in learning should be speedily reinforced, or wrong ones as speedily corrected, do not meet with ready acceptance by all teachers in higher education. There seems to be a prevalent feeling that students are mature enough to wait for their corrections; but, although they may be expected to wait with patience, the evidence is that in any learning prompt feedback leads to greater efficiency.

This is, of course, one of the advantages of programmed learning and of courses designed systematically on similar principles for individual use by students. Some of these have been described earlier in the text (eg Blunt and Blizard, 1973; Brewer, 1974; Witters and Kent, 1972; Sullivan, 1974) or will be mentioned in discussing assessment of courses (page 96).

Various methods have been devised, or arrived at intuitively, which provide feedback to every student on his recall and understanding of informational material, or test his grasp of principles and how to apply them, and these have been found extremely effective (Beard, 1967b). Such methods normally include:

(i) questions for students to answer (eg short answer items, multiple-choice questions, short problem or brief essay questions);

(ii) immediate provision of correct answers or discussion by students of their answers and opportunity to look up further information, putting any outstanding questions to the tutor;

(iii) correction of the students' records for use in revision.

The tutor may also set practical work depending on the information gained, or recommend further related study. These methods have the double merit that the students can assess their own learning and retain corrected records, whilst the tutor obtains feedback on the effectiveness of his teaching from the students failures, questions, or enthusiasm for further enquiry.

A possible advantage of continuous assessment is that it can provide feedback which assists students in improving their future performance, but this depends on the skill of teachers in making informative comments. The Open University has had to produce books of advice for tutors, illustrating how to give effective feedback on essays (Grugeon et al, 1972).

There are few published accounts of continuous assessment so far. Carpenter (1975) reports that when continuous assessment was used throughout the year in industrial studies, mechanical engineering students put more time and effort into their exercises, making regular and frequent visits to staff for enlargement and discussion of various topics. However, where only a third of the assessment was continuous, for the electrical engineers, this made little impression on motivation. Generally students put greatest effort into aspects of assessment carrying the greatest weight. It is the view of Bailey, Beynon, and Sims (1975) that continuous assessment is particularly appropriate in the first year undergraduate course.

Elton, too (Elton et al, 1970) reports the value to students of receiving lecture notes and self-testing devices. Students read and revised more and could follow lectures better. Provision of full lecture notes in a basic science course for first year undergraduates brought benefits to staff as well, for they saw for the first time what their colleagues were teaching and were able to integrate courses. Although notes were provided in advance, lectures were well attended and students expected their lecturers to talk around the subject.

The difficulty with large classes is to establish an efficient organisation which maintains close personal contact between staff and students (cf Donaldson, 1974). Bent (1974) tried to solve this problem in physical chemistry by introducing the Keller Method while retaining lectures for one aspect of the course. MacManaway (1970) discarded lectures, substituting lecture scripts and giving questions and assignments designed to test students' comprehension and to extend their thinking in sociology. Feedback was first obtained by substituting discussion in seven or eight groups of three or four students during the first half-hour of lecture time, and then by general discussion and elucidation when leaders reported their groups' findings. Ninety percent of the students found the method stimulating and enjoyable, 93 percent commented on the value of discussions, 64 percent said they had learned to use sociological ideas and terminology and only 13 percent preferred some kind of lecture; but 58 percent still said they felt uncertain what information was important.

Television seems an unlikely medium for the use of audience participation and feedback to the student, but Gane (1969), having presented his objectives on the screen, gave information and then asked a question or posed a problem. A carefully-judged length of time was allowed for each viewer to work out his response before the answer was given on the screen and discussed. If the problems are carefully chosen — as in a programmed sequence — the student's answer book should provide a valuable record of key issues. This technique may also be used in a lecture, but in both cases subsequent discussion to remove misconceptions is advisable.

Teather and Marchant (1974) claim that an experiment designed to test effects of cueing, questioning and providing knowledge of results, shows that the last of these is most effective. That cueing — by alerting students in advance to questions they should be able to answer — may be effective only under some conditions was shown in an experiment by Coombs (1974): cueing made a significant difference only when students were already fairly knowledgeable. Possibly, expectancies promote learning only after a critical level of background knowledge has been reached.

Applying information is also an aid to retention. McLeish found that students recalled only 42 percent of the content of a lecture immediately afterwards but, if they received a copy of the lecture and applied its contents soon after hearing the lecture, they retained three-quarters of what they had learned after one month (McLeish, 1968).

III: ACTIVITY IN LEARNING

The importance of activity on the part of the learner is a principle of learning as it is described by the field psychologists. They describe learning in terms of the individual sizing up, or interpreting, his world in a way that is meaningful to him, integrating experiences into existing organisations of knowledge and using the environment in ways advantageous to him. It follows that what the individual perceives is selective. In teaching, therefore, field psychologists are concerned with motivation, stress the importance of arranging that learning experiences are organised into meaningful wholes, and favour the use of problem situations which enable the learner to gain 'insight' as he suddenly realises how to use information or how to interpret it meaningfully. In addition, the learner may develop and follow his own goals. Their more self-directed, problem-centred approach may be thought of as most suited to practical laboratory work or in teaching students to work independently by providing problems or topics for them to study alone; but it also aids recall and retention of information, probably because in the course of the student's activities he integrates information meaningfully into what he already knows. This makes it easier to retrieve when it is needed since many bonds have been formed with other knowledge. Holland et al (1968) used practical experience to make clinical students aware of social and emotional aspects of medical care by assigning each student in the experimental group a patient from the ante-natal clinic to visit and attend during the following seven months. These students also prepared reports on such topics as family size by social class within the area, etc, while the control group followed a conventional course. In a multiple-choice test given unexpectedly, both groups did about equally well in clinical obstetrics but the experimental group was significantly superior in knowledge of social medicine.

It is relevant here that one of the main criticisms of the lecture by medical students is that it is a passive method of learning (British Medical Students Association, 1965). Many of them wish a large proportion of lectures to be replaced by teaching methods allowing more student participation, and, in the lectures that remain, they advocate a more extensive use of audio-visual techniques so providing for simultaneous auditory and visual learning.

Mental activity is normally associated with high arousal. The hypothesis that high arousal during the acquisition phase of learning results in good long-term memory was supported in an investigation by Lavach (1973) using five groups of students who listened to a 20-minute taped lecture, where in some cases 'arousing' words were used preceding selected passages. Recall scores supported the arousal/retention hypothesis. According to this hypothesis performance may be impaired either by over-arousal, as in the case of over-anxiety, or by low arousal associated with sleep or fatigue. Fatigue can be of many kinds (Miles and Bramley, 1974). Local fatigue should be distinguished from general fatigue because the student should apply different strategies to deal with them. Cumulative fatigue, possibly resulting from overwork, is more serious and takes longer to remedy. Conversely, in one experiment anxious students performed better in a test-like situation when music was played as they entered than when there was either silence or music throughout the test (Stanton, 1975). Music may have been beneficially relaxing at first, but an interruption later.

In contrast, there is some evidence of the value of relaxation in learning. Repin and Orlov (1967), reporting experiments in an Australian journal, claimed that when 2-3 hours were allowed for conventional learning some 70-80 percent of 50 new English words were recalled on the average immediately afterwards, with a range of 40-100 percent; but, in a state of relaxation, 20 minutes sufficed for students to attain scores of 80-88 percent, and after a further five minutes of visual rehearsal this rose to 92-92 percent. Three months later 90-94 percent of words learned in relaxation, but only 50-60 percent of words learned conventionally, could be recalled by the students. Special suggestion to memorise improved performance further. The editors comment, however, that it is difficult to assess the experiment as full information is lacking and there were no statistical tests.

The importance of activity on the part of the student is also one of the tenets of those who design programmes for machines and programmed books. Influenced by the behaviourist school of psychology they concentrate their attention on changes in overt performance and describe learning as built up by reinforcement of responses to stimuli from the environment, though these may, of course, be consequent upon the learner's activity. The learner should therefore be encouraged to follow a logically organised sequence of stimuli, including questions, with feedback as to his success serving to reinforce correct responses.

IV: STRUCTURE IN TEACHING AND LEARNING

Although it is commonly believed that it is easier to follow and to learn from well-structured lessons and courses, especially in sciences, few investigations have been made to compare different ways of structuring subject matter in teaching.

Diggins (1974) outlines a sequential presentation of the properties of haemoglobin in the form of a 'concept map'. He has attempted to arrange the concepts into a hierarchy after the manner of Gagné (1965). This leads to a consideration of prerequisite knowledge in biochemistry and raises the question as to what is relevant for the understanding of advanced concepts by medical and para-medical students. He summarises some evidence pertaining to the use of Ausubel's 'advance organisers', suggesting ways in which their value might be investigated. He also suggests original papers which would be suitable for discussion with students and so could be used to test Epstein's method of teaching (1970, 1972).

Levine (1974) discusses the use of models in teaching concepts in chemistry: for instance the Rutherford, Bohr, and Schrodinger models to teach atomic structure. He considers that a logical step-by-step sequence is needed, avoiding models for which students are not ready, those which may interfere with what they already know, and those that will clash with subsequent teaching. Since this and Epstein's approach are radically different there seems to be a case for exploring their relative success, taking into account students' past knowledge and their preferences for different modes of learning.

In an experiment in Canada, Sullivan (1974) found that the performance of students learning for a highly structured course was significantly superior to that of students attending lectures and various kinds of group discussion; students on the structured course gained twice as many As and Bs, and correlation with final results proved to be high. However, he rightly points out that generalisation from one experiment is dangerous, for the specific method of instruction which is most effective depends on the nature of the subject matter and the characteristics of the learners. Other findings in the effectiveness of structured courses will be mentioned later in discussing assessment (Chapter 6).

V: PROGRAMMED LEARNING

a. Comparisons with other methods

A number of studies show that programmed learning is at least as effective as traditional teaching. When Orr (1968) tested sailors for the retention of information about atomic structure one day, one week, and two weeks after tuition, there was no significant difference between those taught by programmed learning and those taught by conventional lectures. Farrell (1965) found a notable increase in retention of information, giving a 49 percent lower failure rate for the programmed learning group, in an examination in the Royal Canadian Air Force.

In these cases the topics were fairly elementary; yet at degree level, programmed learning appears to be almost as successful. Hoare and Inglis (1965) used programmes in chemistry with first year MB students who reported that they found them 'useful', or 'very useful', for increasing comprehension, revision and answering problems. The class as a whole did exceptionally well in the organic chemistry examination. In a further study with first year MB and dental students, Hoare and Revans (1969) used objective tests based on Bloom's (1956) First Three Levels of Objectives. Compared with a pre-test they found that students' knowledge of facts, theories and formulae increased 70 percent, their ability to use them increased 50 percent and their ability to apply them in new or unfamiliar situations increased by 43 percent. Performance of individual students at the different levels indicated that ability to recall knowledge and power to apply it were relatively distinct abilities. Using 268 university students, Pikas (1969) compared programmed learning with traditional teaching in which the students had to ask the questions, and for additional teaching where the students were passive listeners. By immediately testing some students on their factual knowledge and its application, and testing the others on its application the next day, he found that programmed learning was superior for immediate tests of factual knowledge, while traditional teaching was superior where the students had to answer questions of application; but there was little difference where the traditional teaching required the student to be a passive listener. Both kinds of traditional teaching were superior on tests of application given the next day when compared with programmed learning. Unlike Hoare and Revan's Programme, the one used by Pikas did not require students to apply the knowledge they had learned. Pikas argues that the greater the dissimilarity between the learning and task situations, the greater the superiority of traditional teaching. We may conclude that if one wishes students to apply the information they learn one must teach them to do so.

Guild (1966) has reported the successful use of a programme for individual
teaching in dentistry. Jamieson, James, and Leytham (1969) compare programmed learning, lectures well augmented with visual aids, and 'straight
lectures' given to 184 postgraduate students in educational psychology. Post-
tests showed that significant differences in learning were still apparent on a
test five months later when there was no apparent difference in the effect of
the two styles of lecture. At no stage was there a significant correlation
with the students' intelligence, sex, estimated teaching ability, or arts/
science background. Buckley-Sharp et al (1969) found programmed learning
groups significantly superior to a group given introductory notes in a test of
biochemistry administered three weeks later. In another enquiry in chemistry
(Hogg, 1973), a majority of students found programmed texts very useful;
those who did not complained that they were 'dull and boring' or 'too time-
consuming'.

b.   Branching programmes

A linear programme is a single ordered succession of frames — usually
statements with a word missing — and proceeds by very easy stages. The
answer to each frame is provided either at the beginning of the next one or
overleaf. Since there is no provision for the correction of errors the programme must necessarily consist of short steps which are easy to answer
correctly. A branching programme offers a choice of answers and students
proceed to different frames according to the answer they select. They are
told whether they were right or wrong, and why. Thus they proceed by
different paths and at different speeds. In branching programmes frames
may be fairly long.

The advantage claimed for branching programmes is that they provide feedback specific to the needs of individual students. But Stones (1967) has
argued that since "all the branches and remedial sequences are related to a
hypothesised best linear path", and feedback in linear programmes can be
amplified beyond mere confirmation of a correct response, there is no
important difference between the two forms of programme. Senter et al (1966)
found that only six percent of the possible 'wrong' branches were used with
Crowder's original programme, 'Arithmetic of Computers'. Kaufman
(1963/4) found no significant difference in the amount of remedial material
between the two kinds of programme. When Biran (1966) and Biran and
Pickering (1968) 'unscrambled' a branching programme, it took less time to
do with no decrease in learning. The answers to questionnaires showed that
sixth form and adult students prefer a straightforward presentation. Biran
suggests that searching through a scrambled book may hinder learning, while
this is avoided if a machine is used; but three out of four studies reviewed by
Tobin (1968) showed no significant advantage in machine presentation of
branching programmes. Tobin concludes that the major variable affecting the
success of the programme is the quality of the original cluster analysis and,
while the machine can act as an attention-focussing device for younger and
less able students, machines are no better than a programmed text for the

average student. It is possible that branching programmes have a particular role where the objective is to improve students' powers of judgement (Peel, 1968). Tobin's conclusion is confirmed by Owen et al (1965), who, in a carefully designed experiment, compared a branching programme in electro-cardiography with a course of lectures specially prepared to correspond with the programmed material. They found no interaction between method and academic ability, nor between method and sex. Less able students profited most from using teaching machines, but the women in this group did better when taught by lectures. Overall, the two groups spent about equal times in study, but the majority of students preferred machines to lectures.

c.   Programmed learning and individual differences

In a survey of the available literature on programmed learning and personality, Dallos (1975) found that high IQ level was related to lower error rate, higher attention level, and less time to complete tasks. Whereas in children high anxiety correlates positively with achievement, the opposite seems to be the case for adults and students. Students with low anxiety scores do best (Shadbolt and Leith, 1967; Knight and Sassenrath, 1967). Leith and Wisdom (1970) found that adults scoring low on neuroticism achieved more overall on a 'reception' programme (one with maximum structure and guidance) than on a 'discovery' programme. Introverts also performed better on structural linear programmes but extroverts did better on discovery programmes (Leith and Trown, 1970; Rasheed, 1967).

Contrary to the majority of findings, Dallos (1975) reported a positive correlation between success in programmed texts and creativity. Madill (1975) classified a group of engineering students according to the degree of concrete/abstract thinking they employed. The students were assigned to three groups with different motivational conditions to study a programmed text. Abstract thinkers responded differently according to the kind of motivation employed. The academic behaviour of students midway on the abstract/conrete continuum was like the behaviour of concrete thinkers. In an experiment by Knight and Sassenrath (1966) students having high 'need for achievement' performed better than others on linear programmes; but Morris et al (1970) found that although undergraduates having 'high need for achievement' worked faster than other students, they made more errors. Apter and Murgatroyd (1975) have also studied the speed at which students work through a programme. Of the many patterns of pacing, the most frequent involved working more slowly at the beginning and end than in the middle. There was no overall correlation between speed and error rate. Extroverts worked slightly more quickly, but there were no differences between the sexes or in other individual variables.

As one might expect, there is some evidence that programmed learning is a good 'leveller'. Castle and Davidson (1969) found it useful with overseas students who may have had language difficulties and concluded that programmed learning was "effective to bring groups of people varying widely in social, ethnic and backgrounds in a new medical faculty, to the same high level of

attainment" at the beginning of a course. Using linear and branching programmes in an HNC course in chemistry, Glynn (1965) found that they liked
the method and did well on compulsory questions in their examinations. The
weakest students made the greatest gains.

d.   Reservations with regard to the principles of programmed learning

When the effectiveness of a teaching method has been shown to vary with such
a wide range of individual factors it is not surprising that any all-embracing
principles on which the method is based can only be held with reservations.
In recent years several authors have written on the decline and fall of the
principles of programmed learning (Leith, 1969; Bligh et al, 1975). In
particular Hartley (1974a) has summarised findings of the previous 20 years
relating to these principles.

Available evidence seems to sustain the principle of feedback, but while the
principle of small steps has had some early support and seems to be
suitable in subjects with an in-built logical structure or a difficult language,
it is less important at university level and is best with students or children
who are beginners at a subject or who are low in confidence.

The principle of employing a planned sequence of instruction may be theoret-
ically important, but randomness in periods under two hours seems to make
little difference, perhaps because students can manipulate this quantity of
subject matter and thus individual preferences and background knowledge are
more influential. Hartley suggests that surprise sequences are more motiva-
ting than logical ones, and if the sequencing of information is important we
might have expected more differences to appear in comparisons of branching
and linear programmes.

The principle of self-pacing does not seem to be supported in all cases.
Students do not always know what pace is appropriate and there can be administrative problems resulting from contrasting speeds of working. On the
other hand group pacing is difficult to set up. There appears to be conflicting
evidence on whether programmes are best studied individually, in pairs, or
in larger groups. James Hartley (1968) has argued that although self-pacing
is an important principle, individual work is sometimes not as effective as
working in pairs. Dick (1963) used a programme on algebra 3,500 frames
long with 34 university students, and found that individuals worked more
quickly and, although there was no difference when tested at first, students
who worked in pairs scored better on a test one year later. Since, apart
from two experiments (Amaria et al, 1969; Amaria and Leith, 1969), work
with schoolchildren does not show the same results, it is tempting to
speculate whether age, intellect, or co-operative abilities are important
variables. James (1970) used a branching programme on management with
individuals and with unpaced groups of three or four apprentices or managers
and, although the short term results favoured individual learning, the difference was much less after four weeks. There is some evidence that discussion

methods favour long-term retention compared with presentational methods of teaching, and this may explain the findings of both Dick and James in the context of programmed learning. There appears to be little difference between working individually and in a group larger than three, perhaps because the usual method of displaying the frames for a group by projection onto a screen does not easily permit discussion of each response by the students. Thus it may be the opportunity for discussion that is important, rather than the size of the co-operative group.

In spite of the principle of self-pacing, a number of experiments in which programmes have been presented to a whole group requiring students to keep pace with its other members do not show any significant deterioration in learning. When Moore (1967) used a programme on 53 students of physiological psychology, there was no difference in test results between those who learned in a group and those who worked individually with booklets. Moore argues that although the average time taken by individuals was 77 minutes and by the group 87 minutes, group presentation has advantages if programmed learning is used in class where all must wait for the slowest. James Hartley (1968) reviews a number of studies, comparing individual usage of a booklet with film strip or tv projection of an algebra programme to a group. Most showed no significant difference between the two methods. But Gallegos (1968) found that both high- and low-ability students learned better if they did programmes at their own speed, or were paced at a speed lower than the class average, than if they were made to go faster than usual. Stones (1966), who experimented with programmed learning to see whether supervision, working in a group, or working to a set time influenced results or attitudes, found no differences between five groups except that students working independently took more time.

The importance of activity when learning has already been mentioned in a previous section. Leith and Buckle (1966) cast an interesting light on this principle when they studied the effect of overt and covert responses to frames in relation to the difficulty of their subject matter. Following the use of a programme in electronics with three student groups formed on the basis of prior knowledge (A level physics at least, O level at least, or little knowledge of physics), they concluded that the more difficult the task was to the learner, the greater was the need for overt responses. But, in line with the well-known finding that rote learning is more efficient when it takes place vocally than only mentally, they found that overt responses were in general more effective than covert ones. The traditional reason for this is that overt responses are more strongly reinforced than covert ones, but this has usually been tested by requiring some subjects to make overt responses and not others. When Sime and Boyce (1969) in an important and well-design experiment only required overt responses on some of the material subsequently tested, they concluded that the questions in a programme raised the level of students' attention, because non-reinforced concepts were also learned better when questions were asked about something else.

An interesting experiment by Wright (1967) challenges the principles of activity and small steps. She designed an experiment in which undergraduates worked through a section of a programmed text on psychology prepared in one of four ways: short frames with blanks, paragraphs followed by questions, and these two conditions again with the answers filled in. Completed frames proved significantly more effective than those with blanks, and paragraphs were significantly more effective than frames, paragraphs with questions being by far the most effective. She suggested that the structure of the material was more clear in paragraphs. Williams (1963) confirmed the importance of making a written response, but Krumboltz (1964) found no significant difference between students using a conventional programme with written responses and those reading prose, in either immediate or a delayed test. In an earlier experiment (Krumboltz and Weisman, 1962) he found superior recall in the response group after two weeks.

e. Programmes with other methods

Stavert (1969), Stavert and Wingate (1966), found that a course based exclusively on programmes resulted in ten percent lower test scores and unpopularity of the method compared with conventional teaching; but popularity, test scores and motivation improved when a variety of techniques including tutorials and laboratory work were used. He concludes that programmed learning must be part of a system of instruction which allows for human interaction. Croxton and Martin (1965, 1968) replaced courses in strength of materials and theory of structures by two series of short programmes together with problems and tests to follow each programme. The programmes were progressively modified according to difficulties recorded by students on a standard form. Their students preferred being taught both subjects this way, finding them fairly easy whereas formerly they were amongst the most difficult; but they wished contact with their tutors to be maintained, and wanted some competition from other students. Problems and difficulties were therefore considered in tutorials six days after receiving the programmes, and lectures were replaced by tests on which the student had to score 90 percent before receiving the next programme. The time spent on these courses, as compared with others, suggests that the tests, the pressure to be ready for tutorials, and the inclusion of test results in their final assessment increased motivation.

A number of studies have compared different methods of programme presentation. Using Owen's programme, Stretton, Hall, and Owen (1967) compared the use of teaching machines and programmed textbooks, and found that the machines took insignificantly longer and there was no difference in their effectiveness. Conner (1968), teaching engineers, also found no difference, but groups using machines and programmed texts both did better than controls in the annual examination. Tobin (1968) summarised 19 studies comparing machine and textbook presentation of linear programmes and found one to the advantage of each, and seventeen where there was no significant difference. Using pairs of matched students, Poppleton and Austwick (1964) compared a programme in elementary statistics with reading and note-taking and found

no difference in learning by either method. Moore (1967) compared the use of
an individual programmed booklet with a programme presented frame by frame
onto a screen for a longer time than it took 60 percent of the class to respond.
He concluded that the group method can save time in conventional teaching
situations, requires only one programme, is cheaper than individual machines
and can be used as part of a conventional lesson. However, this requires
the presence of a teacher, whereas individual work with programmes does not.

James (1970) compared a programmed videotape plus a handout with the use of
an instruction booklet. Students preferred the videotape, but their learning
was marginally better with the booklet. Comparing a tape-recorded presentation of a programme on the operation of machine tools with a similar written
version, Amswych (1967) found the oral presentation both quicker and more
effective.

VI: THE LECTURE

a. Function

Inquiries in connection with the Hale Report (University Grants Committee,
1964) show that the views of university teachers in Britain on lecturing are
more favourable than those in the medical students' report (British Medical
Students' Association, 1965). Most of them believe that students are too
immature to study independently and that lectures are the most economical
way of communicating information to them. Scientists, in particular,
regard the lecture as an excellent way to introduce and to open up difficult
topics which students cannot undertake on their own, while it is generally
felt that the lecture is the only solution to a paucity of books or rapid
developments in subject matter which outdate existing books. Nearly all
teachers claim to cover the syllabus in broad scope and principle, using only
sufficient illustration for the principle to be understood. They point out also
that they can respond to the students in a way that teaching aids cannot, that
they are able to show their students how to organise a topic or how to build
up a complex argument or diagram, and that they can share their enthusiasm
for the subject, include discussion of recent developments or indicate
topics for further inquiry. However, in studying anxieties of new lecturers,
Ellis and Jones (1974) found that giving lectures caused them more anxiety
than any other form of teaching; in consequence, they developed defence
mechanisms such as use of jargon or of a prepared script, distortion to hide
ignorance, being dogmatic, submissive, over-critical or too theoretical,
and relying excessively on empirical evidence or histrionics.

The comments of students consulted in Marris's inquiry (1965), that they
desired lectures to be clear, orderly synopses, logically planned,
emphasising basic principles and with not too many digressions, and that
time should not be wasted in imparting the contents of the text-book, suggest
that lecturers may be less successful than they believe in using lectures to
impart knowledge in these ways. The high percentages of students (over 40

percent) commenting adversely on delivery and clarity of exposition tend to confirm this. On the other hand, there is evidence that some students share the lecturers' more favourable view of the lecture. In the study by Joyce and Weatherall (1959) comparing four methods of teaching, the students considered lectures outstandingly the most useful, demonstrations following some way behind, with seminars a close third and practicals a close fourth. But students of the Royal Dental Hospital School of Dental Surgery in their opinion poll on lectures showed less agreement (Students' Society Committee, 1966). There was no consistent view as to the value of lectures, nor as to how courses might be improved. The only conclusion which could be drawn with confidence from this part of the inquiry was that more lectures would be unpopular. There was no doubt, however, that students of the School expected lectures to fulfil three functions: to introduce the subject and set it in its context, to bring the text-book up to date, and to provide discussion of problems and their possible solutions.

In the NUS report of 1969 (Saunders et al), students thought the major functions of lectures were to impart information (76 percent), to provide a framework for the course (75 percent), to indicate methods of approaching the subject (64 percent), to indicate sources of reference (47 percent) and to stimulate independent work (41 per cent). They criticised the hindrance to understanding necessitated by note-taking, frequent repetition of standard text-books, and poor preparation and presentation. Distribution of duplicated notes by the lecturer was strongly advocated to overcome the first of these.

Maclaine (1965), in surveying teaching methods in Australian universities, grouped the advantages and disadvantages under these headings: motivational, organisational, and informational-elucidatory. In addition to listing most of the points made in the Hale Report he included under the first heading exploration of desirable by-ways, under the second, guidance in reading and evaluation of text-books, and, under the third, "to explore and clarify ideas and techniques". But an adverse effect of the comprehensive course of lectures in an Australian university school is mentioned by Schonell, Roe, and Middleton (1962) who comment that although teachers may sincerely believe that their lectures serve as a guide to reading they are, in fact, used by some students as a wholly self-sufficient course of study; in their survey, 15 percent of Queensland students relied almost entirely on lecture notes and the majority of students studied primarily from them.

It may be noticed that all these enquiries used expressions of subjective opinion. With the exception of Joyce and Weatherall (who found a conflict between subjective opinions and objective tests), none conducted controlled observations to test their opinions. Furthermore, they scarcely distinguish between what lectures can achieve and what they usually do.

Accordingly Bligh (1975b) set out firstly to test the validity of students' opinions, and found that their judgements of how much they had learned in lectures bore no consistent relationship with how much they had learned as measured by objective tests. Secondly he used objective tests at eight cognitive levels to evaluate lectures in psychology. Tests of terminology, facts, general principles and simple comprehension showed comparable gains; skill in applying knowledge showed varied increases while improvements in analysis, synthesis and evaluation of information were negligible. Furthermore, although it might be expected that students with previous knowledge and comprehension of the subject, as measured by a pre-test, could use the occasion to think more deeply about it, they did no better than others in the post-test on questions requiring higher levels of thinking.

These findings suggest that lectures can best be used to convey information and that they are not occasions during which much thought occurs, at least as they are currently organised. However, this inference is open to the criticism that it confuses cognitive level with cognitive difficulty. The results of this experiment could have been obtained if the questions at a high cognitive level happened to use more difficult concepts. Subsequent experiments confirmed that there is a critical level of difficulty, which varies with the ability of the students, at which the choice of teaching method may make a big difference; but since difficulty was shown to increase with cognitive level when the subject matter is kept constant, the criticism is not a severe one.

Some idea of whether lectures usually do teach higher cognitive objectives than other methods can be obtained by surveying the comparative literature. In spite of its resources, this is something the Hale Committee failed to do.

Bligh's survey (1972a) of a large number of studies in which lectures were compared with other methods — mainly in the United States — suggests that whilst lectures are as good as other methods of conveying information, they are less good than group discussion, independent study, or 'student-centred' teaching in developing thinking or in changing attitudes. A finding which perhaps lends support to this is that of Houston and Pilliner (1974), who compared the effects of different teaching styles on the level of thinking attained by older pupils in schools. They found that teachers who employed an 'open-ended' style (ie allowing discussion, and responding to pupils) were more successful in promoting complex and higher-level educational objectives than were dogmatic/expository teachers. Hornsby-Smith (1973) explains unfavourable attitudes towards physical sciences (contrasted with life sciences) in terms of the teaching styles which predominate. He concludes that expository science teaching styles must be replaced to a significant degree by more heuristic teaching styles. An experiment by Morstain (1973) indicates some benefits of increased self-directed independent study.

Thus the fact of students gaining information without learning to think, can be partly a consequence of the choice of teaching method; but the presentation of lectures may be modified in response to students. Zillman and Cantor (1973), contrasting lectures containing rhetorical questions and their answers with alternative versions omitting the questions, found that listening to the questions significantly enhanced learning and recall of facts. Womersley, Stenhouse, and Dunn (1974) used multipe-choice questions during the course of each lecture to encourage students to think and to structure the information they received. Their investigation found that student performance was better in tests after lectures if they had been questioned in this way. A number of investigators have used mixed methods rather than a lecture (Bligh, 1974; Linacre, 1973).

An extensive survey by Costin (1972) or research into lecturing versus other methods reaches no clear conclusions, owing mainly to poor design of the experiments, for variables were confounded and little was measured except information gained.

Whether lectures should be compulsory or not is a matter to be decided in the context of the aims of the school or department. In some schools encouragement of independence in students is valued so highly that some inefficiency is countenanced as a result of absence; but that absentees from lectures do less well in tests and examinations than those who attend has been shown in several studies (Adams et al, 1960; Holloway, 1966). Indeed, one investigation found that attendance at lectures and seminars was by far the most important correlate of examination success in social science (Preston, 1975). Where it is impossible to make good the loss of information in lectures, compulsory attendance would generally be recommended.

b.   Place and length

The place of the lecture differs in the various faculties. In 1964, at the time of the Hale Report, arts faculties used mainly lectures and discussion groups, together with reading, whereas in the science faculties there were more lectures with practical or laboratory periods but comparatively little discussion. In arts the average weekly hours spent in lectures were 6.8 from a total of 10.1 hours of instruction, in pure science 8.3 of 17.3 hours and, in applied sciences, both lecture time and total time spent in instruction were still higher viz 10.7 and 19.6 hours (University Grants Committee, 1964). During the last few years, however, there has been a considerable increase in the use of small discussion groups in departments of science and mathematics (Beard, 1967a).

In law there is a similar trend. A survey of legal education in 1966 shows that the majority of lecturers agree that some lectures are essential, but they would welcome the extension of the tutorial system to at least two tutorials per week (Wilson, 1966). They also consider that students should have more opportunity to sample law in action in courts and solicitors' offices, subsequently discussing their visits.

There is little experimental work on the lecture from British sources. Holloway (1966) compared recall of information in dentistry among groups of first- and third-year students attending lectures at 9 am or 4.30 pm. Analysis of scores in two ways, comparing students with themselves on different occasions, or students with each other in the same test items, showed significant superiority for classes held in the morning. Bligh (1974) found lectures at 9.30 am more effective than those at 11.15 am.

McLeish (1968) was interested in the problem of whether students listening to 40 minutes or one hour of a lecture would remember less of it than those who were present for the first 20 minutes only, due to interferences set up by later material. He used three experimental groups who attended different lengths of lecture and a control group who did not attend. Overall the experimental group recalled 42 percent of what they had heard as measured by an objective test immediately afterwards, but the hypothesis that there would be loss of recall due to retroactive interference was not borne out. This may perhaps be explained by a difference in content of the three parts of the lecture, but further experiment is needed to determine in what ways later material may vary before it causes retroactive interference. In theory there should be minimal retroactive interference with the final part of a lecture, and this receives some support from an experiment by Johnston and Calhoun (1969). Using a short tape-recorded talk and multiple-choice questions with 269 students, they found that material at the beginning and end of a talk was better remembered than the central sections no matter in what order the information was presented. In the experiment by Trenaman, quoted by McLeish, listeners to a 45-minute talk on astronomy assimilated appreciably less after the first fifteen minutes and, after thirty minutes, ceased to take in anything additional or forgot what they had memorised earlier. However, it is impossible to generalise from the results of a single experiment of this kind even if we know the subject matter, the manner of presentation, and the difficulty of the subject to the participants. Lloyd (1968) compared the number of facts noted by students during each period of ten minutes during a lecture. He concluded that after an initial increase, there was a steady decline until the last ten minutes, and that those planning lectures should bear this in mind.

Observation suggests that a lecture given at a suitable speed in mathematics or certain science topics, in which a logical presentation is written on the blackboard, provides constant opportunity to the student to obtain feedback on his understanding of the topic; for, unless the speed is too great, he can work out the next line just in advance of the lecturer, obtaining confirmation, or correction, as soon as that line is written. Inability to obtain reinforcement in this way is probably the chief cause of frustration when the lecturer proceeds too fast or presents material in a disorderly fashion.

c.   Delivery

There does not appear to be any British experimental work on techniques of delivering lectures; but views expressed in inquiries have some interest as there is often a high level of agreement. Students of the Royal Dental Hospital School of Dental Surgery comment (Students' Society Committee, 1966): "a lecture has to be delivered very very slowly indeed before the speed is found to be too slow but only a moderate increase in pace will produce complaints of 'too fast'." However, they remark on inconsistencies in views as to suitability of speed in delivering orthodontics lectures: 44 percent of the fourth year, 7 percent of the fifth year, and 80 percent of the sixth year found the speed unsuitable; possibly this reflects the anxiety of students at the approach of an examination, but it may also be affected by the difficulty of the subject at each level and perhaps suggests that speed should vary inversely with difficulty of material. This is consistent with an experiment by Bligh (1974) who gave identical lectures to three groups at different speeds. Results of multiple choice tests at eight cognitive levels showed significant interaction between speed and subject matter on questions requiring more thought, but differences at lower cognitive levels and for speed alone were not significant. There was a critical speed and level of question difficulty at which increases in speed made a crucial difference. Interestingly, he found that tape-recorded lectures could be taken twice as fast as the same lectures delivered by a teacher in person. Speed may also be a factor which influences students to say (NUS, 1969; Marris, 1965) that the major criticism of the lecture method is that 'the opportunity to grasp basic ideas is hindered by the necessity to take notes'. If so, the finding by Gust and Schumacher (1969) that writing speeds of female students are significantly faster than those of their male counterparts has relevance to lectures as well as examinations.

It is generally agreed that a lecture is more effective if it is spoken freely rather than read, and that repetition is helpful in aiding subsequent recall. It is also advantageous to supplement the spoken word by visual aids where these are relevant. But lecturing styles tend to be stereotyped despite the case for variety and enterprise (Bligh(1970a). To help and interest first year students taking a compulsory 'structure and properties of matter' course, Betts and Walton (1970) gave lectures together as a dialogue to nearly 400 students at a time, using television monitors for demonstrations and illustrations in two lecture theatres. Betts provided the logical outline with Walton interposing awkward questions and conducting demonstrations or experiments. They report that although the brighter students might have preferred a more rapid presentation, on the whole the students were favourable. The dialogue lecture merits wider use since differences of opinion can be expressed and contrasting voices maintain student attention. At the same time one may question the widespread practice of obliging such large audiences to listen to the same content despite a very wide range in ability and prior knowledge.

d.   Evaluation

Evaluation of teaching methods in general is dealt with in Chapter 6, but some comments specific to the lecture are appropriate here. It is not easy to evaluate a lecture, taking into account all its objectives, and it would probably be undesirable to attempt to evaluate each lecture of a series. Nevertheless some evaluation appears to be worthwhile. Few of the heads of departments consulted as to the success of lectures in an Australian inquiry were satisfied that objectives were achieved (Australian Vice-Chancellors Committee, 1963).

They commented that lectures tended to succeed with certain students but not with others, or that lectures were more successful in certain subjects than in others. Whereas these differences seem inevitable, students complain of basic faults such as poor preparation, that lectures are neither clear nor systematic, or are so ill-delivered as to be barely audible, or that they are addressed to the professor's notes or to the blackboard. Others report lectures delivered so rapidly that they cannot be followed coherently, consisting of a mass of detail, or presenting a difficult argument in a fashion which only the most able students can follow.

Despite these varied criticisms it is probably true that almost all lecturers sincerely desire that their lectures should be well delivered and readily comprehensible. Failure in these respects is often unconscious and students of undergraduate age often fail to provide the hints, or outspoken criticisms, which would result in improved practice on the part of the lecturer. In the belief that most lecturers would welcome any means of finding out to what extent they were successful, a group of scientists working in a research group with the University Teaching Methods Research Unit of the University of London Institute of Education prepared a questionnaire for use by students. They invited them to agree with various statements, on a five-point scale, relating to the lecturer's audibility, speed and quality of delivery, appearance, manner and rapport with the class, and to aspects of presentation of subject matter or use of audio-visual aids, as well as to comment on surroundings and other factors influencing the success of the lecture. It is of interest that even among these enthusiasts it was not until nearly a year later that any of the group agreed to use the questionnaire; for, as one lecturer said: "It will only give the students an opportunity to make satirical comments." Yet when it was tried at the beginning of courses enthusiastic reports were sent in. A veterinary scientist reported that his students 'seemed grateful that something was being done' and that they combined to give a joint criticism and made useful suggestions. An electrical engineer (McVey, 1967) tried two forms of questionnaire with small groups. He discovered that there was more extraneous noise than he had supposed and that on changing from lectures with notes to lectures without notes he had not slowed his pace sufficiently. He received confirmation of information obtained in earlier surveys that his students liked duplicated notes and coloured diagrams since they found the latter clearer than the blackboard and the former enabled them to concentrate better on the lecture. A biologist received approximately 80 percent response from a large class and felt that it had been particularly valuable to receive criticisms and comments at the beginning of a course since it enabled her to adapt her teaching to their needs in the remaining lectures. Although this technique does not inform the teacher how much the students are learning, it does establish better rapport and almost certainly results in more efficient teaching.

This is one satisfactory method to use, but it is not the only one. Among methods reported within the University of London are the following: taping a lecture and listening to it subsequently in private; taping a lecture and observing in the following class while they listen to the recording; inviting students to provide immediate feedback on the lecturer's success by complaints as to excessive speed, lack of explanation of difficult points etc; and, in a few cases, lecturers invite colleagues to attend their lectures and to criticise them. A number of other methods used in American Schools are outlined in an article by Simpson (1965). Flood Page (1974) surveys the American experience in a recent book. Siebring and Schaff (1974) survey more than one hundred and forty studies. Smithers (1970a) asked 431 university students at the end of their second year to rate 50 possible characteristics of the ideal lecturer. Students in all fields of study were agreed that the ideal lecturer is an authority in his subject and can expound it clearly, that he thoroughly prepares his lectures, gives them an obvious framework, and is ready to respond to questions. In other respects there were differences in emphasis according to field of study: students of applied science and engineering appeared to look towards lectures for information; social scientists, for stimulation. These differences in emphasis suggest that teaching and lecturing abilities may be more specific than is commonly supposed.

Smithers (1970b) also found that extroverts attached more importance to the lecture as a performance; for them the ideal lecturer is entertaining, confident and at ease. Those more 'unstable' as measured by the Eysenck Personality Inventory want the lecturer to be as definite and certain as possible and to give full notes, whilst dogmatic students are most concerned that the lecturer should keep to the point, set clear goals and convey the information lucidly.

In an earlier inquiry by Cooper and Foy (1967), students and staff in a university department of pharmacy were asked to put statements describing lecturers' characteristics in order of importance. The first ten for the students, in order, were as follows:

1. presents his material clearly and logically;
2. enables the student to understand the basic principle of the subject;
3. can be clearly heard;
4. makes his material intelligibly meaningful;
5. adequately covers the ground in the lecture course;
6. maintains continuity in the course;
7. is constructive and helpful in his criticism;
8. shows an expert knowledge of his subject;
9. adopts an appropriate pace in his lectures;
10. includes in his lectures materials which are not readily accessible in text-books.

Staff and student ratings correlated quite highly (0.77); but, whereas students valued adequate coverage of the course, attempts to link theory with laboratory and practical work, even spacing of requirements for written work, and humour, staff were much more concerned with avoidance of excess factual detail. Two-and-a-half years later Foy (1969) repeated the inquiry with a different set of students and found a correlation with the judgements of their predecessors of

0.93 which certainly confirms the reliability, though not necessarily the validity, of students' judgements. Bligh (1974), for instance, has shown that since an easy lecture may be rated as 'good' by weaker students and 'poor' by able ones, whereas the reverse holds for a difficult lecture, the correlation between scores in a test of what they learn and their ratings of the lectures may vary with their difficulty.

VII: AUDIO-VISUAL AIDS

Considering the widespread use of audio-visual aids in university teaching the number of investigations to determine their value in British university schools is rather few. A monograph by Flood Page (1971) reviews the available literature in greater detail than is possible here and the inquiring reader is advised to refer to it. It is true that some advances due to new techniques are so great that experiments are unnecessary to demonstrate them — the transmission of a lecture to millions instead of hundreds, for example — but if the value of the aid is in doubt then experiments are desirable. Unfortunately, where experiments have been made their results are too little publicised, so that the complaint that it takes thirty years for the findings of educational experiments to be put into practice is sometimes fully justified. In 1937, Seymour showed that a light-coloured board with dark lettering was more efficient than the familiar black-board and chalk; both children and adults could read dark blue letters from a pale yellow board some 15 percent faster than chalk letters from a blackboard, while the children could copy from it in 10 percent less time. Nevertheless, it was not until 1966 that manufacturers displayed light boards with dark 'pencils'. Even then they cannot have experimented with them in a sample of schools, for the 'pencils' contained coloured fluids and would have proved irresistible to young artists and aspiring mechanics alike. These findings should be known in university departments where boards are in constant use, eg in the mathematics departments where the new boards would not only save students' time in note-taking but could avoid the deposit of chalk dust commonly found on lecture-room floors. More recently Foster (1968) used slides showing lower case letters and found that the maximum distance for 100 percent correct identification was significantly superior with black letters on a white background than with white on black.

Probably the effect of dark lines on a light background is one reason for the popularity of the overhead projector (OHP): this combines the advantage of the blackboard, that the teacher can construct diagrams or notes as the lesson proceeds, with the further advantage of facing the class so that contact is not lost, and adds the possibility of building up complex diagrams by use of successive, previously-prepared overlays. Apart from an experiment by Perlberg and Resh (1967), quoted by Flood Page (1971), in which the use of the OHP was an advantage in geometry but not in hydrology, there has been little work comparing either its various uses, or its general effectiveness, with that of other methods of presentation. Likewise, few experiments have been traced comparing these methods of presentation with each other, or the OHP with the blackboard. Over a three-year period, Allen (1975) compared three lecture courses using a blackboard, three using a single OHP, and two using a two-channel slide presentation. The slide presentation was more popular with students and Allen appears to infer that it is more beneficial. Certainly the overhead projector offers opportunity to provide an illustration when it is most relevant and without loss of time.

In text-books, proximity of illustrations to the relevant section of the text seems critical. Whalley and Fleming (1975), in an investigation into the attention given to diagrams by a sample of students, found that when diagrams immediately followed the sentence referring to them, students spent thirty-five percent of their time studying them; if they were elsewhere on the same page students gave only fifteen percent of their time on average; whilst if the diagrams were on other pages they were not studied at all. Moreover, where diagrams and reference to them were consecutive, students perceived an article as significantly clearer and easier to understand.

a.   Audio-tapes

Audio-tapes are comparatively cheap and, like television, have some self-evident advantages. In medicine (Graves and Graves, 1963) they enable students to listen to interviews between consultants and their patients which otherwise could be attended by, at most, one student; in conjunction with slides they are used to display the symptoms of diseases for the use of students overseas who lack teachers, or they may be borrowed by general practitioners at home for revision, to acquaint themselves with new developments, or to learn to recognise symptoms of rare diseases (Graves and Graves, 1965, 1967). In all of these cases the increase in efficiency is obvious; but, in university teaching, where a tape may be used to replace a lecture, experiments are necessary to determine which method is more successful.

Using 20 multiple-choice questions testing retention of information, de Winter Hebron (1974) compared groups of students given a traditional library induction course consisting of a lecture, opportunity for questions, a booklet, and a guided tour, with groups given two days to use a tape-slide programme and the opportunity to ask questions. He found no difference. Holloway (1964) compared a formal lecture demonstration of a practical procedure in conservative dentistry with instruction by a tape-recording augmented by colour transparencies, using matched groups from a class of 22 students. No significant differences were found in capacity of the groups to carry out practical work or in retention of information after one month. In so small a sample differences would need to be very great to reach significance even at the five percent level, but the tape-recorder group scored significantly higher in immediate recall of information. Possibly this superiority was due to the conciseness of the tape-recording which enabled students to play it twice during the time taken for demonstrations.

Reduction in time for equivalent learning appears to be an advantage of tape-recorded instruction. In a series of experiments (Bligh, 1970b, 1974), students obtained comparable scores on post-tests although live lectures took about twice as long as identical tape-recorded talks. Students hearing recordings of lectures obtained better scores on multiple choice questions requiring some thought than those who heard the lecture live, or who had the same time to read the same words in a lecture script. A later experiment using audio-tape showed that a slower speed of delivery led to better scores on questions at higher cognitive levels, or near the limits of students' ability.

Fletcher and Watson (1968) provided a tape-recorded commentary to lead four students simultaneously through an orderly microscopical examination of histopathological specimens. Their system includes the use of more than one voice to avoid monotony, sets of slides for each student, and an optional replay device for the classroom with three channels carrying the same commentary, but progressively delayed. This enables students to spend longer viewing one slide and to resume on a later tape. They say the advantages of their system include greater accuracy and clarity of description, standardisation and improvement of the histological examination, ease of revision and editing, active student participation and reduction of irregular, inconvenient teaching of small groups.

One of the advantages of tape-slide teaching is that it can be combined with other methods, particularly laboratory work. The use of tapes or books with information and questions, together with slides, has proved very effective in the teaching of veterinary science (Appleby and Poland, 1968). When Engel et al (1974) used audio-tapes with other supporting material they were as efficient as face-to-face teaching, but less popular. Their popularity is greater when personal contact with others is assured. When Wendlandt et al (1975) compared traditional lectures with a system in which two lecture periods per week were devoted to tape-slide teaching and the remaining period to problem-solving and discussion, two-thirds of the students preferred the latter.

Use of synchronised tape-slide material in a structured programme to assist students in problem-solving was a significant improvement for engineering students (Le Marne, 1972) except for the weakest of them. A package, including programmed scripts, text-books, films, and cassette tapes proved effective in teaching students to appreciate the physics underlying an experiment and to recognise errors of observation (Brandt, Ansell, and Cryer, 1974). Tape-slide teaching has also been used to overcome poor motivation in subsidiary engineering courses at the University of Salford (Andrew, 1975). They are used individually or in small groups and allow more informal use of lecture time.

A chance observation of preference for a tape-recording is mentioned in the Brynmor Jones Report (University Grants Committee et al, 1965): a professor of mathematics prepared a lecture on probability theory in such a way that the mathematics was spoken in detail as it was written on the board in order to tape it for another class; when it was repeated with the other group the lecture proved 'surprisingly successful', the students finding the absence of the lecturer to some extent advantageous.

Tape has the further advantage that it is suited to individual use. A student who finds a topic difficult can repeat it until he know it, so avoiding constant requests to his teacher for help or interruptions to a class of students who are already competent. Tapes, with slides, are being prepared for these reasons in several of London's Dental Schools.

At Newcastle a windowless and otherwise non-functional room has been used to supplement conventional teaching methods by the provision of a synchro-nised stereo tape-recorder and slide projector which may be used individually or in groups. The synchrony is obtained by an impulse on the second channel of the tape-recorder activating the automatic projector. Carré (1969) provided audio-tapes in booths to supplement and dovetail with practicals and CCTV lectures, to promote deeper understanding by more able students, and to remedy deficiencies of weaker students or those with less background knowledge. He reports that students were enthusiastic, accepted responsibility for their own learning, and could progress at their own rate. A similar pro-vision for up to 500 students of economic geography, made by Woods and Northcott (1970), included lectures with a linear programme design, visual materials, multiple-choice questions and problems. Nearly all students preferred carrel learning to lectures. They liked to be able to go back over a point, felt more involved and, with a more flexible timetable, better com-munication between staff led to an improvement in the overall course structure. Compared with controls, fewer students using carrels failed, although slightly fewer obtained honours. New devices which make individual operation simpler are being prepared, for example Harden et al (1968) describe a device to record lectures synchronised with slides in an inexpensive and easily modified form. In a later experiment they compared a programmed tape-slide presen-tation with conventional teaching by lectures. Students taught in this way significantly improved their position in class and reacted favourably. Students found they were able to concentrate, the work was 'made easy' and the oppor-tunity to work at their own speed was a particular advantage for those from overseas. However, they commented that the method was 'antisocial', too intensive and lacked humour!

Perhaps the most extensive development of tape in teaching is for use in language laboratories and other language teaching. Many teachers are now engaged in experiments applying the lessons and techniques of modern linguis-tics to the teaching of languages and to discover the best ways of using techno-logical aids. These are listed in the Registers compiled at the Centre for Information on Language Teaching and Research (CILT) (Lunt, 1973, 1976) and in a survey of Research and Materials Development in Vocational Uses of Language (Lunt, 1974).

Materials development based on authentic contemporary language and up-to-date linguistic and pedagogical theory include studies such as that by Biggs and Blanc (Register Code No. 783) who have recorded spontaneous conversations, discussions, interviews and meetings in Orléans, in such a way as to provide a body of material suitable for research and study of the living spoken language, and for applications to the teaching of French at post-intermediate level. Other notable studies are by Ingamellis (No. 1018) and by a Working Party of the Scottish Universities (No. 1593).

Teaching of languages for special purposes is usually achieved by use of language laboratory courses designed for individual study. Some of these are based on behaviourist theories of stimulus response bonds, the concept of reinforcement and maximum motivation, together with applied linguistics and audio-visual equipment. Courses involving research have been prepared by Smith (No. 887), Jelinek (No. 982), Dore (No. 1128), Green (No. 1908) and Hartley (No. 1917).

Research into materials for the less widely taught languages is normally based on a structural analysis of the language. Sloss (No. 1028), for instance, is researching into the development of teaching materials and techniques for modern colloquial Chinese. Other research materials are listed in CILT Language and Culture Guides.

SELMOUS group (Special English Language Materials for Overseas University Students) was formed in 1972 to share experience in dealing with common problems, and to exchange materials and the results of research on English for overseas students. A collection of papers has been published (Cowie and Heaton, 1977). Other researches appear in the Registers under Nos. 1509, 1538, 1832, 1916 and 1961.

Whilst references to the use of the language laboratory and other equipment are distributed throughout the Registers, examples of research projects are provided by McCarthy (No. 1111) and Doble (No. 1416). Doble has been exploring the roles of the language laboratory in the advanced teaching of modern languages. Particular regard has been paid to aural comprehension and the remedial aspects of pronunciation and intonation.

CILT Selected Reading List 22 briefly discusses and lists intensive language courses. These have been developed largely for military personnel and other services and for businessmen.

The effects of residence abroad are reported in a study of German language attainment (Gomes da Costa, Smith, and Whiteley, 1974). Two conclusions of the authors are that there is a considerable disparity between the aims of degree courses and the students' aims (mainly because students wish to attain competence in speaking the language), and that time spent abroad is the most powerful determiner of high-level language attainment. Effects of experience overseas have also been studied in some depth at the University of Bradford (Willis, Doble, Sankarayya and Smithers, 1977).

b.   Television

Comparisons of teaching by television with traditional lectures or other conventional methods do not, at the present time, give a complete picture of
their relative advantages. Summaries of American research (Chu and
Schramm, 1967; Dubin and Hedley, 1969) and comparisons in other countries
(Bligh et al, 1975) suggest not only that television is no more effective in
teaching information than traditional methods, but that its relative merits for
this objective in higher education are probably lower than in any other sector
or age group. Its merits lie in the circumstances in which it can be used and
the widening of the content of courses which it makes possible.. Its existence
changes the objectives that can reasonably be attempted.

Maclaine (1965) describes an experiment at the University of Sydney in which
postgraduate students of education attended lectures, listened to a lecture on
television, or viewed a television demonstration; but no significant differences were found in the students' ability to recall information or to indicate
how to apply it. The impersonality and pace of the TV lecture were criticised,
the demonstration being considered more interesting.

Using restricted technical equipment with students of electrical engineering,
Craig (1968) obtained satisfactory results when prepared notes were issued
immediately prior to transmission, and followed by tutorials. Presentation
was of a high standard, and the medium was not over-used.

Macfarlane-Smith (1968) reports of students in 27 Engineering Science Departments that those who included BBC programmes in a course did better in an
objective test of knowledge, and developed a more favourable attitude to the
subject, than students who followed the conventional courses. He later confirmed these findings, obtaining significant positive correlations between
students' attainments in five engineering examinations and attitudes to their
course, and between their examination and intelligence test scores. Students
of above average intelligence, especially as measured by verbal tests,
showed particular benefit from the programmes as compared with controls.

On an immediate multiple choice post-test Sclare and Thomson (1968) found
that a group taught psychiatry by CCTV did significantly better than one
taught be conventional case study demonstration, but no better than one
taught by programmed instruction. Since the first two groups showed a
favourable change of attitude to the subject, CCTV appeared to be the most
valuable of the three methods.

Experiments in English medical schools in teaching surgery by use of television (Smith and Wyllie, 1965; Smith et al, 1966; Smith, 1974) showed more
benefit from television, particularly to the lower 85 percent of students, and
29 out of 36 students who commented on the value of television as a teaching
method approved of it. Smith notes that all types of students learn reasonably
well from television and that in some circumstances students learn more

quickly than by orthodox methods. The lecturers who use the method observe that students benefit more from TV where it is used as an ancilliary visual aid integrated into teaching, than where it is used as an unaccompanied visual aid.

This raises an essential point. Television is not a substitute for other methods but a supplement to them. Consequently, straightforward comparisons of TV with other teaching methods probably do not have much meaning. Therefore, instead of comparisons, we will now turn to consider how TV is used and what it is used for.

Gibb (1968) tested the effectiveness of a commentary superimposed over a videotape recording of a classroom situation shown to student-teachers. The commentary seemed essential to enable students to see the structure of the lesson, but was less effective in demonstraing teaching techniques and the use of visual aids. Groups who heard the commentary could not apply what they had learned to a second lesson which immediately followed the first. Although this could reflect a limitation of the method, it may be better explained by fatigue since the difference in tests between those who heard the commentary in the first lesson, and controls, grew less significant for items occurring later in the lesson. Answers to specific questions suggest that viewers have a limited capacity to process incoming information and that they tend to ignore auditory information when both auditory and visual information are presented together. Gibb suggests that unless auditory material is compelling, cues taking 0.3 seconds, such as 'notice that...' are needed to give the viewer time to switch to his auditory channel. In general it is wiser to give important verbal information when there is little visual competition. However, the work of Vernon (1953) and Trenaman (1967) indicates that, because visuals hold attention while the acquisition of information is consolidated by words, visual and auditory material should be closely integrated. Problems of fatigue and attention span have been considered by Wood and Hedley (1968), Barrington (1965), and Mills (1966). The general consensus seems to be that programmes should last between 15 and 25 minutes.

In a comparison of different ways of presenting television programmes, Barrington (1971) found plain backgrounds with animated diagrams more effective than sophisticated backgrounds designed to simulate realistic situations. A method of compressing material using animated diagrams and captions led to better scores than cine films, particularly with lower-ability students.

We have previously mentioned the importance of feedback for the attention and recall of information. By using CCTV, James (1970) has shown the value of feedback in the learning of motor and interpersonal skills by apprentices, trampoliners, musical conductors and workers in the social sciences.

Within the last few years, Perrott and her colleagues (1975a, b, c) have developed self-instructional methods for teachers using videotape or film. For example these are designed to help teachers use better questioning techniques following repeated practise and self-observation of a few minutes' teaching. Brown (1976a) has reported a similar technique with university teachers. Ivey (1974) has extended the principle of microteaching to 'micro-counselling'. Trainee teachers were taught selective listening skills and learned to recognise that their role to facilitate pupil activity complements expository teaching. Kallenbach and Gall (1969) report that the use of TV in microteaching saved time and expense, and was administratively convenient. Furthermore, Edwards (1975) found no difference between supervised and unsupervised microteaching when self-instructional materials were available.

Indeed, microteaching is currently the 'in thing'. British research, together with the work of Dwight Allen and his associates at Stanford and Perlberg at Haifa, has been favourable. It is therefore salutary to remember that Copeland (1975) found no significant difference between experimental and control groups in the tendency to use the desired teaching skills, and concluded that "microteaching can be assumed to have no significant relationship with the subsequent classroom performance of students".

Nevertheless in Copeland's study student teachers increase in confidence and awareness of personal habits. Wood and Hedley (1968) and Perrott and Duthie (1969) have reported mixed reactions from student teachers viewing their performance in the classroom, weaker students being less favourable and more snesitive. Others (Hale, 1965) found it difficult to assess the general class atmosphere from TV. Mills (1966) and Wood and Hedley (1968) report improved understanding of teaching techniques from demonstrations; but Mills, like Gibb (1968), found no significant improvement in their application to classroom situations. While accepting the effectiveness of microteaching, Bligh et al (1975) question the value assumptions that underlie it. They argue that because the appropriateness of any given teaching skill varies, its adoption into a teacher's style is not necessarily an improvement.

Television is the only visual aid which can form a living link between different institutions or different sections of the same institution. Not only can very large audiences be reached simultaneiously, but experiences are accessible which could normally be observed by only one or two people at a time or in which the presence of even one observer could act as an interference. For example in medical schools, closed circuit television now enables large numberts of students to view an operation when it takes place, or subsequently on videotape, to view a single specimen under a microscope, or to observe a specialist's interview with his patient. In the third edition of this book we reported a link between a medical school and a public mortuary and the linking of five medical schools in different parts of the country for a pathology seminar (Special Correspondent, 1966a, b). In Glasgow closed circuit television was used to link colleges of education and schools to enable student teachers to observe classes in action with a minimum of interference from their observation. At Cambridge several language classes have been taught simultaneously by using a monitor in each of 30 booths in a language laboratory.

Bennet (1968) has described the use of CCTV at Cambridge in teaching first year students to read at a fairly fast pace while listening to a recording of the text. The use of television by the Open University is, of course, well known and will not be elaborated here.

In Edinburgh Cowan, McConnell, and Bolton (1970) substituted a carefully designed programme including CCTV, discussions, lecture notes, unstructured practical periods, and 'open tutorials' for formal lectures and tutorials to achieve students' objectives such as (1) lucid expression, (2) profitable independent technical reading, (3) answering and asking specific questions, and (4) accurate observation. The ratio of staff to student contact hours was 20.5:1 compared with the UGC average ratio of 13.8:1; yet group interaction and staff-student contact were better than on the replaced lecture-tutorial system. Examinations showed more spontaneous syntheses of material from various subjects. The authors concluded that even with large classes the objectives and methods were feasible, efficient and attractive to students.

To overcome problems of staff shortage Robertson (1969) used videotape recordings of modified conventional lectures in engineering. Information was written on cards displayed around the studio for ease of following them with the camera in a sequence. In the same way a shortage of laboratory assistants persuaded Pantaleo (1975) to use videotape instruction and he claims that it required less production time than and similar cost to tape/slide presentations. At many universities videotape machines are intensively used in laboratories and are available on library shelves (eg Brunel University: Noordhof, 1974). Library videotapes may be used for revision, to clarify difficulties, or to permit an absent student to catch up.

Ten years after it was written, the report of the Research Unit of the National Extension College is still apposite. It comments: "...the use of closed circuit television in appropriate departments is rapidly becoming standard practice in British universities;... the use of lectures and demonstrations recorded by one means or another is already well established in some of them;... there is a modest but increasing traffic between departments; the idea of creating a permanent network of links for the exchange of 'live' television material between a group of universities...has serious administrative and financial drawbacks... the exchange of recorded material at present offers an altogether more flexible way of pooling resources and from the technical point of view calls only for apparatus which will be equally valuable for intra-university purposes."

Possibly the greatest contribution to efficiency in teaching is that of film and filmstrip for they can be sent to groups who lack teachers, or can be used for private study. However, the number of British experiments in connection with conventional teaching in higher education is small. An extensive, carefully designed investigation into teaching in the Royal Navy was made by Vernon (1946) comparing classes taught with the aid of film or film strips. Seven main types of instruction were used combining the methods in different ways. Closely comparable improvements in examinations, averaging about eight percent, resulted from the use of the film strip, from the addition of the film, from good versus poor instructors, and from high versus low intelligence in the classes. Those improvements were highly significant statistically. The film was perhaps most successful since it took less time than the strip; when shown in conjunction with the strip it aided comprehension rather than memory for details. The film, or film strip, could largely compensate for weakness among instructors, but the taking of notes was of little value.

Kenshole (1968) prepared a film loop and a tape with slides to teach three-phase alternating current theory, in place of the usual six one-hour lectures. This did not lead to any significant improvement in attainment by first year students but resulted in a significant saving of time of 40 percent.

Ash and Carlton (1953), who studied the value of note-taking during film learning, found that it appeared to set up interference with viewing which was not wholly compensated for even when time was given subsequently to review notes.

The efficiency of film in conjunction with other methods has also been demonstrated in the teaching of physiology (Steinberg and Lewis, 1951). Showing of the film increased knowledge in both groups of students appreciably but was most effective after prolonged preparation; however, their teachers doubted whether the additional time spent in preparation was worthwhile. Differences in the projection method have also been shown to influence learning. Teather (1974) compared front and rear projection of film and CCTV, using material originally designed for CCTV, and found rear projection most effective. Physical factors involved in viewing and the novelty value of the projection method are discussed in relation to this finding.

No experiments have been traced with film loops or with automatic slide projectors although some interesting pieces of apparatus and related materials have been prepared for use in teaching. Film loops lasting two or three minutes each have to be devised to illustrate a succession of concepts, so enabling students to use them in any order or to select only those of special interest to them. In the case of the slide projector accompanied by tape, or written statements of what to observe, it would be interesting to know whether questions and subsequent answers would result in better retention of material than would statements. Experience in programmed learning suggests that a challenge to the student to make response, with immediate correction of his answer, would be far more effective than the relatively passive method of telling him what to look for.

The use of computers in British higher education is in its infancy but has grown fairly rapidly during the last five years. The availability of cheap pocket computers now makes their use an everyday activity in calculating and in working through various kinds of computing programmes. Flood Page reported in

1971 that fifteen to twenty higher education institutions were considering, or trying out, the use of computers for teaching purposes. The Centre for Educational Technology (CET) has made suggestions for the future direction of research. Dr R.A. Wisbey has used a computer at Cambridge for the selection and grading of language materials. De Dombal, Hartley, and Sleeman (1969) report the use of a computer to teach the techniques of clinical diagnosis to medical students. It can provide facts about a 'patient' and respond in answer to questions. When the student enters his diagnosis by teletype, the computer indicates any errors and invites the student to try again. The intention is to help students to see the significance of findings and guide them so that they proceed logically, eliciting information fully at each stage — an objective common to many subjects. Although it cannot teach skills with patients, the method seems to have the approval of students and to teach effectively. Harrison (1968) has described a number of developments such as a computer linked to a teaching machine in a mobile classroom. This can provide a record of each student's progress, modify instructions in accordance with an individual's previous responses, give continuous evaluation, and serve a large number of students simultaneously. Grubb (1968) presented a 'map' of a statistics course on a cathode ray tube to mature students. They chose which section they wished to tackle, and an IBM 1500 computer routed them through the course. Motivation was improved and a record of student choices could give information for the design of future courses. Computer-based learning is increasing particularly in physical sciences and mathematics. Its use is discussed by Abbott, Cook, Hartley, and Rawson (1972) and a number of innovations are described. A full evaluation was then in progress. In a polytechnic, students of catering use a computer to analyse and design menus (Forsyth, 1973). Lekan (1970) has prepared an index of computer-assisted learning and Hawkridge (1974) discusses problems in implementing computer-managed learning.

Other electronic aids are mentioned by Mr J. Martin at the University of Kent at Canterbury where electronic equipment is used to increase reading effectiveness in foreign languages. At the Faculty of Technology in Manchester, electronic scanning gives access to library material at a distance.

A five-year National Programme for Development of Computer Assisted Learning has just been completed (1977), but so far its published reports have been disappointing for their lack of rigorous evaluations.

CHAPTER 4   SKILLS AND ABILITIES

A wide variety of skills and abilities is required in learning at the university level, ranging from mechanical and manual skills, in which one procedure must be learned and repeated accurately, to higher mental abilities, such as skill in solving unfamiliar problems, where flexibility in thinking and capacity to consider unexpected possibilities play a considerable part in success. Different methods of learning and teaching are required in these cases, but an essential in learning all skills is that the student should have adequate opportunity for practice and should receive information as to his success.

I: MECHANICAL AND MANUAL SKILLS

Learning of mechanical and manual skills has not been studied experimentally among university students although there are a number of interesting innovations in teaching.

In industry, however, fairly extensive studies have been made in the teaching and learning of skills. Many of these are described by Seymour (1966). Some of the findings have relevance to practical skills learned in certain university courses such as the filling of a tooth, dissection of a cadaver or assembly of electrical circuits from diagrams. Seymour distinguishes the 'knowledge' and 'skills' content in learning a practical task. The former involves memory for symbolic material in the form of words, numbers or diagrams, which is said to be learned when it has been memorised and can be recalled appropriately; the skills content involves non-symbolic information and its acquisition requires motor and perceptual learning. If the knowledge content can be readily memorised, the control of the motor activities can proceed unimpeded. Difficulty arises when diagrams and written texts have to be consulted as the task proceeds or where the level of discrimination required is near the threshold for that particular sense. This difficulty is overcome in learning skills, such as dissections, where instructions are played on audiotape which the student can stop at will. Coyle and Servant (1975) have occasionally used film instead of conventional practical work. Learning does not seem to have been impaired and the method was no less popular with students. Alternatively, a tape dealing with the entire process, emphasising difficult points, seems highly effective. In a personal communication, Dr Goodhue of the Biology Department at Trinity College, Dublin, reports that tapes, together with diagrams and other illustrations he has prepared, have proved so successful in teaching first-year students to dissect rats that their initial attempt which formerly took three hours, with many errors (after a demonstration), are now completed almost perfectly in one hour (Goodhue, 1969).

Experiments suggest that it is wasteful initially to practice too intensively. Henshaw et al (1933) did an experiment with three groups of 30 subjects employed on chain assembly for 80 minutes each morning. In the afternoon, Group 1 did another 80 minutes chain assembly, Group II practised a different operation and Group III did no assembly, yet the performance of the three groups remained almost identical; but it is a common experience that rest periods improve performance — in learning to drive a car, for instance, or in learning to swim. Seymour suggests that the optimum period of practice initially is half-an-hour, extending to two hours when the individual is already practised.

An observation in many of the more complex skills is that the learner reaches plateaux, where he appears to make little or no progress, but that these are followed by rapid improvements, possibly owing to the synthesis of a number of skills. Whether the skill transfers to another task seems to follow from the extent to which it depends on selecting similar groupings of activities of the muscles, and the skill the individual shows in 'selectivity', ie in more frequent selection of optimum responses. Of interest here is a finding that in learning to type, students who began to learn on an electric typewriter later attained greater speeds on a manual typewriter than those who learned to use the manual typewriter first. Thus initial 'pacing' by the machine had a lasting effect (Garbutt, 1963).

Contradictory results have been obtained in studies of learning by part or whole methods. Woodworth (Seymour, 1966) favoured the 'whole' method with special attention to and repetition of difficult or important parts. This may account for Goodhue's success since his method consists in showing the whole dissection, but with coloured diagrams for critical stages. Experiments at Birmingham University Department of Engineering Production (Seymour, 1966, Ch. 8) suggest that a more useful distinction is between perceptual content of different parts of the task than between 'part' and 'whole'. Results of one experiment suggest that task elements with difficult perceptual content require longer training and that, therefore, methods which enable greater attention to be concentrated on these elements are advantageous.

The experiment of Wilcox (1974) on the teaching of two kinds of serial task of three lengths is, perhaps, more artificial. He used backward chaining (ie learning the last step first, then the last two, the last three etc until the whole was learned), forward chaining, and the whole method. The tasks involved were a motor task-paper-folding and numerical procedures, which may not exactly parallel any learning task in industry or university. Although it has been claimed that backward chaining would be most effective, its sole advantage in this experiment proved to be when working with a long number chain. In general, the 'whole' method was superior to either chaining method.

As in other fields, knowledge of results leads to more rapid learning; what is needed is an exact and prompt indication of what went wrong and the direction from 'wrong' to 'right'.

II: LABORATORY SKILLS

How far the development of skills is an objective in laboratory work is a matter of opinion. In the Electrical Engineering Department at Salford University both staff and students thought the purpose of laboratory work was to consolidate learning from lectures, to stimulate independent thought, to communicate, and to acquire experimental techniques; students wanted laboratory work to be open-ended and easily applicable to vocational engineering (Carter and Lee, 1975).

Since increasingly complex laboratory work cannot be tackled effectively by students lacking essential laboratory skills, some teachers are providing initial skills sessions. Black, Griffith, and Powell (1974) set tasks for students following brief explanation from the lecturer. Typical problems involve estimating the growth of a hair in metres per second, estimating the number of atoms lost from the sleeve of a coat when rubbed across the table, or the number of grains of salt in a salt cellar. Students work in groups of four, discussing their ideas. Attention is given to translation skills, eg from graph to verbal description, scaling up or down, and first steps in planning a project are discussed. Leckey (1972) has developed a course to give students skill in modern instrumentation together with appreciation of limitations imposed by inaccuracies of particular instruments. Neither course includes evaluation to determine how far students have actually acquired these skills.

III: STUDY SKILLS

The term 'study skills' is here used to cover all such skills as speed and comprehension in reading, note-taking or methods of learning from notes and books. Thus they are essentially verbal skills, but do not include oral skills, verbal fluency or literary style. In universities there has been a tendency to take such skills for granted. Exceptional slowness in reading may be remarked on, but it is not usually thought of as remediable. It is rare to find a university teacher who makes a point of exploring his students' methods of study and guides them to use more efficient techniques.

Yet the few investigations which have so far been made suggest that this is one area in which considerable advances could still be achieved. The effect of a course of study methods for Zambian students (Bethlehem, 1973) was that they gained significantly in their second year compared with a control group that did not receive advice and tutoring. Seminars did not significantly benefit first-year students, but did so for second, third, and fourth years. Scores on study questionnaires correlated more highly with grades for students in Zambia than in Britain. Van Zoost and Jackson (1974) found that a study-skills course resulted in improved study habits with continuing improvement for at least six months, but students' monitoring of their own study behaviour had no significant benefit. This may seem to conflict with a survey of investigations into self-directed study groups, which suggested that study methods and skills in learning are greater in self-directed, than in teacher-directed, groups (Beach, 1974). Advantages were noted in the quantity and quality of study: in students' communicative and interpersonal skills, their sense of responsibility for their own growth, their improved critical thinking, their awareness of how study material could be applied, and their lasting curiosity aroused by learning. A possible interpretation is that awareness of one's own study methods in necessary, but insufficient, for improvement; knowledge of alternative methods is also necessary.

Malleson et al (1968) enquired into methods of study of medical students by asking them to record for each period of private study a number to correspond with eight different study methods. Malleson also investigated a number of attitudes and was tentatively able to identify certain factors in study, eg (1) syllabus oriented: pressured vs easy going, (2) methodical vs enjoyable, (3) self-confident vs anxious. Crown et al (1973) compared students who attended their college health centre with controls and concluded that study difficulties are associated with psycho-neurotic and motivational factors.

Comparatively recently, attention has been given to speed and comprehension in reading and to the possibility of teaching students or adults to skim in reading. Barclay (1957) used films specially prepared to increase reading speeds with 61 graduate students drawn from various professions, in an attempt to see whether reading speed could be increased while at least maintaining the level of comprehension. All students made increases in reading speed ranging from 7 percent to 213 percent, and averaging 81 percent. An overall improvement in comprehension was also observed and, after lectures on methods of skimming and scanning, the group achieved a substantial cut in the time taken to find facts. Although this and the succeeding experiments are encouraging, there is probably need for more extensive experiments to determine to what degree the skill is retained and whether it applies only with materials similar to those used in the initial experiment. If this proves to be so, further experiments should be undertaken using more varied materials in training the students.

Hill and Scheuer (1965) used a rapid reading course for medical students, prepared by Fry (1963a, b) with 13 senior pathology students. In their case, reading speed increased on the average by 110 percent, individual improvement ranging from 36 percent to 241 percent. Comprehension was slightly raised and satisfactory speeds were reached in skimming following an exercise in the middle of the course. Although Francis, Collins, and Cassel (1973) found that reading improvement schemes resulted in gains in speed (which were greater for students learning from books than for those using a speed reading projector) this tuition had no effect upon examination performance.

A summary of many similar investigations undertaken among eight experimental populations has been made by Poulton (1961). In the 66 groups who took part in such experiments, mean gains in reading speed range from 11 to 148 percent while those in comprehension lay between -20 and +89 percent. In cases where performance was re-tested some time after the experiment, individuals differed considerably in their capacity to maintain gains, some deteriorating almost to previous levels whereas others almost entirely maintained their new high levels.

Following a review of recent literature, Wright (1968) suggests that efficient reading involves three stages: a preview which is often achieved by skimming, fast reading of the passage, and a review. She quotes Alderman (1926) who found that exercises designed to increase the reader's ability to organise what he read resulted in greater improvement in a comprehension test than exercises intended either to develop vocabulary or to increase retention. She considers that the most important characteristic of written information is its structure and that the reader must restructure difficult material to provide his own 'cognitive map'. Perhaps this is why instructions to summarise or to copy when reading failed to assist students (Howe and Singer, 1975), for even summarising may have added nothing to the students' understanding. And interference with learning occasioned by recording activities proved insignificant unless this requirement imposed constraints on students' learning strategies.

Another investigation of interest, because it should lead to greater understanding of how students study and so lead to better means of guiding them, is that of Jahoda and Thomas (1966). In a pilot survey, 20 individuals were asked to study each of three passages — an introduction to cybernetics presenting a rigorously logical argument; a history text requiring memory for relatively unfamiliar names; and a text on clinical psychology in common sense terms — until they felt they had learned it. They were then asked to compose questions which would adequately test whether a person had learned the passage and were themselves asked questions designed to test what they had learned and at what level of abstraction. During the course of study their progress from page to page was recorded. It proved that techniques differed widely; rapid scanning followed by study of selected passages, perhaps repeatedly, a careful first reading checking back only on a few important passages, constant referral to earlier paragraphs, and so on. Some of them used identical strategies on each passage, whereas others generated strategies appropriate to the material. Questions set by members of the experimental sample in some cases dealt wholly with details, while others concentrated on principles. As a result of this pilot study alone, the authors consider that staff time spent early in a course on individual tutoring, encouraging students to examine their learning processes, could save time later and increase the students' range.

A more recent study by Francis, Collins, and Cassel (1973) contrasted: (a) training in reading involving a speed reading projector; (b) a similar course without mechanical aids; and (c) a conventional reading course without special training. Students receiving the first two treatments improved, the non-projector group acquiring greater speed but not greater comprehension.

Freyberg (1956) has experimented with several methods of note-taking, but these were imposed by the experimenter. He used four methods with parallel groups of students: taking notes, writing full notes, making an outline, or accepting a duplicated summary. His findings suggest that these methods are effective for different purposes: where material was to be recalled very soon but was not required for examinations, taking no notes proved most successful; if it was to be examined, learning from duplicated notes gave the best results. However, the experiment is a limited one. Further experiments would be required to show how these different methods influenced students' learning and study skills over a longer period, and prior discussion with some students of how to take notes more effectively might substantially influence results of the experiment were repeated. The effect of dictated notes has also been investigated by Gilbert (1975) who concluded that "note-taking need not interfere with comprehension of a lecture even when the student is required to take verbatim notes which he has no opportunity to review". However, many more experiments would be needed to determine whether this result held good for other subjects; and, as in all experiments which deal only with average results for groups of students, one cannot say how individuals are affected.

Hartley (1976) has explored the relationships between design of lecture handouts and students' note-taking practices. In five experiments he looked at the effects on note-taking of: (a) the presence of a handout; (b) deleting items in order to provide more space on a handout; (c) increasing the amount of space between items on a handout; and (d) omitting words and phrases on the handout for the student to insert during the lecture. He found that students varied their note-taking practices according to the design of the handout, and in general students having no handout did worse. Students made comments such as "I use them as a basis for notes to which I add information: if time"; "I like to make notes independently and use the handout to check the accuracy of my own note-taking", and "I read them through again after the lecture and can remember much more. Good for revision before exams"; "Very good for revision and understanding..."; "I don't usually find that a handout makes me concentrate, but concentrating on filling in the spaces on this handout encouraged me to pay attention.

Hartley and Cameron (1967) investigated note-taking by recording the number of items in a lecture and checking how many of these were mentioned by students in notes. Rather less than one third of what was said was transmitted to notebooks, but this included about half of what the lecturer considered important. References, definitions, names, and words written on the blackboard were recorded, but experiments leading to theory were omitted. The method suggested that the students regarded the lecture as a framework of ideas and theory in which to fit subsequent work; all reported that they would do subsequent work but only 3 of 22 students did any. The authors conclude that a weakness of the lecture system as a teaching method lies in the discrepancy between the students' stated and achieved objectives; they suggest that the lecturer should reconsider his own objectives, possible ways of attaining them, and techniques to measure their achievement.

In a later study, Hartley and Marshall (1974) unexpectedly in the ninth week of a ten-week course asked students to give in their notes. They report that the general standard of note-taking was extremely poor. On average only 11 percent of the units of information were recorded, the range being from 3 to 129 units out of 520. In immediate recall 'good' and 'poor' note-takers did equally well, but after revision, the 'good' note-takers improved significantly more than the 'poor' ones. They suggest that students should be given instruction in note-taking and that lecturers should indicate when to take notes.

However, Howe (1974) questions the value of note-taking when there are so many inexpensive alternative ways of reproducing knowledge. He suggests that note-taking may influence learning directly, by maintaining attention, and by providing a record which is of particular value to the learner. He asserts that learning is strongly influenced by the particular note-taking strategy an individual adopts; but this is not investigated.

Ability skilfully to collect, collate, and apply information increases in importance with the rapid growth of knowledge and number of specialities. It is an essential component in the capacity to respond flexibly to change. Since it tends to be taken for granted by those teachers who unthinkingly repeat courses and methods used by their teachers in more stable times, too many students are provided in lectures with almost all the information they need for examinations. They therefore have little incentive to develop this skill. Yet they not only need to learn to use libraries effectively but also to use aids which will become more common during their professional lives, such as tape and slide sequences or computers. Fortunately there is a well-established trend to increase activities which put the onus on students to collect information for themselves.

Stahl et al (1975) have devised a self-help learning system in biostatistics using programmed texts, an abstract service, small group discussion and tutoring where available. The pass rate was good and students with no previous experience were no less successful than others.

In any course of teaching method heavily dependent upon reading materials the choice of typographic style is important. At the Open University MacDonald-Ross and Waller (1975) have suggested that the decision on this practical problem should be preceded by criticism of available styles, establishing alternatives and testing them. The use of typographic styles to distinguish different kinds of content has resulted in significantly higher scores on immediate tests of comprehension when readers were told to use the SQ3R study method (Coles and Foster, 1975). In this method students are required to survey a text, ask pertinent questions, read, recall, and revise in that order (Robinson, 1961).

MacKenzie (1974) has shown that Open University students in remote areas performed no worse than others in terms of dropout and degree success, in spite of having no television and counselling services. Research projects are set for a growing number of undergraduates and these and long essays take the place of some traditional examination papers. Librarians are often invited to advise students on the use of library facilities; but few seem to realise that informing students is not enough. At Bradford University Crossley (1968) set exercises for students during a short course designed to ensure that they gained skill in searching literature. This resulted in a higher level of library inquiry and increased use of inter-library services. Wood (1969) also mentions exercises during a course of a similar kind. An enquiry at Sheffield University found that on the average students spent little more than one third of their grant for 'books, stationery and equipment' on books. Although roughly two students in five thought the stock of bookshops was poor or very poor, a similar proportion had never ordered books not in stock. Bristow (1970) held seminars to improve reading, note-taking and reporting among mature teachers studying for a Diploma in Education. These students benefited from the comments of their peers, in addition to those of the group leader, so improving their performance considerably. Steedman (1974) found that lectures on information sources combined with a literature-search exercise received a favourable response from students, who made a much better start to the final year project than students who were not treated in this way.

Essay writing and the writing of laboratory reports are other skills which tend to be taken for granted by university teachers. In 1968 one lecturer in London University mentioned how poor essays were in the final examination of his department; but, in reply to a question, he admitted that the students were not required to write a single essay during their three-year course! Evidently their teachers were making two assumptions, both of which we would consider unjustified: firstly, that students would have the skill to write essays despite lack of practice, and secondly, that answers in essay form were appropriate to test understanding or skill in a subject which did not require verbal work of this kind while learning it. This may be a common error: Beard, Levy, and Maddox (1964) noted a high correlation between scores in a verbal test and an engineering drawing examination, and commented that the examination was probably unnecessarily verbal in content. Because middle-class students use more structurally complex syntactic sequences, more uncommon qualifiers, and fewer fragmented or repetitious word sequences, Pool (1971) believed that students' habits of speech and writing are established well before puberty. Consequently verbal tests will normally discriminate against working-class students. This effect is likely to be increased in courses lacking verbal practice.

Inquiry suggests that the amount of feedback students receive on writing
varies enormously. Although it is obviously the intention in the old, and
and some new, universities that tutorials should fulfil this function, complaints by students indicate that this is not apparent to all tutors as some
spend the time in giving a mini-lecture instead of initiating discussion about
students' work. In London, where staffing does not usually permit individual
tutorials, group discussion of essays is used in some departments, notably
geography. Often a students is asked to read his essay to the group who then
comment on structure, handling of material, use of illustrations, and so on.
At the postgraduate level, Woodford (1972) outlines scientific writing exercises designed for PhD students, who learn to write journal articles, being
encouraged to clarify their thinking before considering an outline, and to
study the requirements of suitable journals. They discuss presentation of
tables, examine drafts for logical flaws or errors, and consider ways of
improving style in writing. Wason (1970, 1973, 1974) outlines various ways
of assisting students. Whilst there can be no doubt that help of these kinds
improves performance, neither author has evaluated his method.

Soloff (1973) has confirmed Kandel's finding (1936) that handwriting influences
grades awarded for the content of essays even when some marks are alloca-
ted for handwriting independently. Two recent studies have shown that
continuous assessment tends to result in more consistent study habits and a
more uniform performance by students throughout a class (Carpenter, 1975;
Bailey et al, 1975).

Where written reports are required there is evidence that students can be
helped to improve them considerably in the course of learning. Dr A.P.
Prosser (Imperial College, University of London) set experimental problems
to pairs of first-year engineering students who were required to solve the
problem and discuss their solutions in some detail with the tutor before
writing their reports (Prosser, 1967). He commented that the reports were
technically of higher quality and more comprehensive after the introduction of
this method, and that marked improvement could be observed during the year
in describing and interpreting results. Although it is fairly generally agreed
that putting one's ideas on paper is an aid to clarity in thinking, the way in
which it clarifies has not been investigated; it is almost certainly in part
because inter-relationships too complex to hold in mind can be seen more
readily when spelled out or arranged diagrammatically, but no doubt the
effort to find the right word to express a half-framed idea in itself leads to
greater clarity. Since it is one of the most important skills it deserves
investigation, both as to how different individuals set about it and how teachers
can aid students in improving their techniques.

IV: ORAL SKILLS AND GROUP DISCUSSION

Oral skills have always been important in medical and dental professions
because doctors and dentists must communicate with colleagues and their
patients. In the legal profession too, oral skills have always been an essen-
tail requirement to elicit information or to exercise persuasion. But,
particularly since the Second World War, proliferation of committees has
increased the need for oral skills among engineers and scientists, while the
use of television and other audio-visual aids has increased the use of oral
communication and at the same time made audiences more critical. Consequently, not only must students develop a capacity to present a report, or to
engage in discussion with experts in other fields, but, as in all communication,
they must appreciate factors which influence decisions, such as interaction
between members of a committee, their difficulties with subject matter, their
prejudices, and so on. Like doctors or lawyers, young scientists must learn
to express themselves well and should gain at least practical experience, if not
theoretical knowledge, of group dynamics. Indeed, by using techniques such
as interaction analysis, doctors are still developing new methods to teach the
skills required in doctor/patient relationships (Scott et al, 1973).

Partly owing to the influence of the Hale Report, the activities of the Nuffield
Foundation, and UGC sponsorship of teaching innovations, the use of group
discussion methods has considerably increased in university teaching during
the last few years. The chief purpose of discussion differs from subject to
subject. In biology the most important purpose is probably encouragement of
critical thinking. In mathematics students may discuss their difficulties.
While younger students of engineering are more likely to discuss problems of
a mathematical nature, older students are more frequently concerned with
applications of engineering to industry (Beard, 1967a). In most subjects,
particularly the humanities, there are occasions when a student gives a talk
on a prepared topic and leads subsequent discussion. In this way students may
learn to play different roles within a group. To develop the variety of skills
required for these roles Bligh (1973) has advocated the use of a progression of
small group methods gradually increasing in size and in the capacity of their
tasks. A later publication (Bligh et al, 1975) recommends a sequence of up to
16 different techniques beginning with small tutorless groups, such as 'buzz
groups', through case studies, class discussion and seminars to methods
requiring and teaching emotional sensitivity such as free group discussion,
T-Groups, and counselling.

Two examples from recent literature will serve to illustrate the use of tutorless groups. Loewenthal and Kostrevski (1973) describe an experiment in
which engineering undergraduates were given exercises in pairs, requiring
them to describe objects to each other. The group who had this training
became superior to a control group, not only in describing objects, but in
their scores on the verbal section of the AH5 'intelligence' test. Smith and
Jepson (1972) used an 'information game' in which students, working in groups
of seven, were each given only part of the findings in a case of metabolic

disease. When left to their own resources of reading and group discussion to answer questions and work out the remaining findings, they argued about a wide range of biochemical reactions with evident enthusiasm and enjoyment. Another investigation related learning during group discussion to the number of leader/student and student/student interactions, and to assessment of students' abilities and intelligence. Only the number of student/student contacts was highly correlated with cognitive gains (Palmer and White, 1974). Niether personality scores, nor numbers of interactions with group leaders, correlated significantly with measures of learning. A recent American experiment (Securro and Walls, 1975) also shows the relative ineffectiveness of teachers, compared with students, in increasing the flow of group discussion. Students who recorded their own and one other student's contributions in discussion, significantly increased their number of contributions. They spoke more than controls and than a group who knew their contributions were being recorded by their teacher.

The majority of studies of group interactions and of group discussion have been made in the United States; but there is a growing volume of contributions from British authors. Klein is the author of two books (1961, 1965); Sprott (1958) surveys many studies, both British and American; Abercrombie in The Anatomy of Judgement (1965) discusses factors which influence judgement and accuracy of observation. In Aims and Techniques of Group Teaching (1970) she relates group methods to objectives and outlines a series of meetings planned to help students to come to terms with the problems of changing status in the authority-dependency relationship. Some of this work will be discussed further in the section on teaching for change of attitudes; but here we are concerned with group dynamics independent of objectives in teaching. There is general agreement that some of the important variables are seating position, talkativeness, personality of the participants, and the kind of leadership. Position proves to be more important than casual observation suggests. The leader's position, if he sits separate from the group but facing them, indicates that he expects members of the group to address him but not each other; if he sits at the head of a table this suggests that he expects to be addressed a substantial part of the time; he must sit among the group as a member of it, or outside it as an observer, if he wishes the group members usually to address each other. Individuals within the group tend to choose positions according to whether they wish to talk or not, preferring a place opposite the leader if they wish to talk to him, but adjacent to him otherwise; a member opposed to the group may withdraw his chair from the circle. Generally, members tend to address those who face them more than members placed adjacent to them. A teacher may use this to encourage a quiet member to talk by placing him opposite a talkative one, or quieten the talkative by placing them next to each other or to the leader. Persistently-silent members may be assigned an active part by preparing a paper or a few points to begin the discussion, while the over-talkative one can be silenced by inviting him to be group secretary or by thanking him for his contribution and inviting other comments on the points he has raised.

Klein (1965) observed that in a series of free discussions members tended to establish characteristic interaction frequencies, high interactive sub-groups being formed, particularly in pairs. In line with American findings she found that the more voluble members tended to be popular and that agreement on the ranks of members increased as the series proceeded. American studies have shown also that it is the talkative members who can most readily get the support of the group. A normally silent member giving the best solution of a problem fails to get it accepted without the aid of one of the most voluble participants. Tuckman and Lorge also found (1962) that contributions by members of low status were normally ignored in arriving at a group solution to a problem; in such a case the solution arrived at by putting together the best points from all individual solutions excelled the solution of the same individuals when working in a group.

Deutsch (1949) studied the effect of giving different information as to the assessment of group work to members of different groups. Some groups were told that they would be assessed collectively, in co-operation, while others were informed that each individual would be assessed independently, in competition with other members of the group. The 'co-operative' group showed more co-ordination of effort, diversity in amount of contribution, sub-division of activity, attentiveness to fellow members, mutual comprehension and communication, and greater orientation, orderliness and productivity per unit time, as well as more favourable evaluation of the group and its products. Berkowitz et al found (1957) that, in groups of three students who were evaluated favourably or unfavourably for contribution made, those groups in which all members were unfavourably rated were most integrated and most highly motivated, while those in which members received different ratings found each other less attractive and were least motivated. Thus, in both cases, elements of competition and perceived difference in achievement were destructive of group spirit and achievement within the group. Personality may have a similar effect; Haythorn et al found (1956) that students of a markedly authoritarian personality were more aggressive and less effective in group discussion than those who were rated 'egalitarian' on the California F-scale.

Contributions of a discussion leader as compared with an observer have been studied by Maier and Solem (1952). They found that minorities obtained a better hearing in a group having a leader and tended to be sheltered by the leader, so that minorities with strongly expressed, but wrong, views continued to hold them in groups with a leader, but were forced to change their views and to accept a correct solution in leaderless groups. This suggests that free group discussion with an observer may be more effective in encouraging critical thinking than discussion in a group with a teacher; but the scope of the experiment is inadequate for anything more than a suggestion that this may be worth investigating further. In an experiment with 800 groups of different sizes, Davey (1969) concluded that a permissive style of leadership was most productive with groups having four to seven members, but that a controlling style was more effective for fewer than four or more than seven.

The value of discussion between students in the absence of a lecturer does not appear to be recognised generally in university courses. Students consulted by Marris (1965) said that they frequently discussed their work with each other and could be less inhibited with staff absent; it was a more satisfactory way of dealing with difficulties since they felt that seeking help from staff was viewed as a confession of incompetence. Teachers who have organised work so that students discussed questions together in pairs, or small groups, before raising further questions with them have found the method very successful (Beard, 1967b).

It was suggested earlier that if students know the objectives on which they are to be assessed, they are more likely to strive to achieve them. However, some objectives are difficult to describe. To let students evaluate the work of their peers is one way of teaching these objectives by experience. American research has found good correlations between peer and teacher evaluations, but self evaluations by students have tended to be generous (Parker and Kristol, 1976; Burke, 1969; Bligh et al, 1975). After reviewing the literature on peer teaching, McNall (1975) concludes that it can improve interpersonal attitudes in the classroom.

V: HIGHER MENTAL SKILLS

a. Critical thinking

'Critical thinking', 'scientific thinking', and 'understanding' are terms which come readily to the minds of teachers when they are asked to outline their chief aims in teaching. However, it is commonly added that many students are very limited in their capacity to think critically. Medical students are often mentioned as a group 'less able than most honours students' who, due to poor ability, are dependent on their teachers, unable to learn without considerable guidance and who, moreover, must be enabled to recall a mass of information before it is possible for them to begin to discuss intelligently or to deal with problems. Teachers who argue in this way would do well to study the findings of psychologists who have investigated the factors operating in transfer of training.

Thorndike (1913) in the earlier phases of these investigations concluded that only identical elements of content, or pattern of procedure, could be trans-ferred from one learning situation to another. In the case of medical courses, for example, some procedures in pre-clinical subjects are relevant in related post-clinical work, and to this extent habits of work transfer directly and beneficially. But transfer applies equally to undesirable habits: learning by rote without understanding, accepting rather than challenging authoritarian statements, and concentrating on accumulation of facts rather than interpret-ing them or making decisions, are also likely to be transferred to the post-clinical course if they have been the pattern of behaviour in the pre-clinical school. Since recent work suggests that more generalised training may be transferred when there is a similarity between the new situation and the one in which the behaviour was learned, it seems imperative to provide a situation in which students are encouraged to be critical as soon as possible. Thus teachers who insist that medical knowledge can be introduced by means of problems which require initiative and understanding in the students as they solve them, are more likely to train doctors of a critical habit of mind with capacity to educate themselves.

Information as to how to be critical may also be required. Connors (1972) describes an experiment in which mature students read an article, 'Decision Making in Britain', at first with little criticism, but when they received further material including an introductory article on 'how to sift and clarify the evidence', they came up with a list of burning questions to put to the authors of the text.

A useful concept is that of 'sets' which consist of expectations based on past experience. In an experiment in the psychology laboratory students attempt to obtain stated quantities of liquid from combinations of three given amounts. The first four problems can be solved only by subtracting the second from the first and adding the third. The fifth problem can be solved in this way but also, more easily, by simply subtracting the third from the first amount. By no means all of those who attempt the problems see the easy alternative. They have developed a 'set' which is useful while conditions remain the same but which is inhibiting so soon as they change. Individuals differ in their flexibility in situations of this kind, those who normally welcome ambiguity and novelty being more likely to hit on the more economical solution. Teachers can use methods which develop flexibility in thinking by fostering 'sets' of a constructive kind, for instance by teaching strategies for attacking problems rather than, or in addition to, 'sets' for specific types of solution.

A constructive use of 'set' is made in teaching French literature in one department of London University (Uren, 1968). A preliminary discussion takes place around the theme of the text to be studied, and students are asked to predict points that the author has made. It is not uncommon for students to bring up in this way all the points touched on in the text before they have even heard it. They are encouraged by their own display of knowledge and listen to the text very attentively to see how it treats the theme. Their tutor takes the opportunity to point out the value of their adopting a similar strategy in their personal reading.

Psychologists would also expect students, like children, to succeed best where teaching methods arouse most interest and most activity on the part of the learner. With children, evidence already exists that retention of information is at least as good when it is gained as a by-product of solving problems as when inculcated by efficient teaching of information only. No doubt this is partly because the information becomes organised into a meaningful whole which, as we have seen, aids retention. Further, the method is likely to inspire so much interest that the children spontaneously follow up the problems, thus extending their range of learning. However, we cannot say categorically that teaching students through problems is more efficient than other current methods, in terms of inculcation of information, for no experiment has been carried out at their level comparing this method with others.

That there is an essential difficulty in thinking objectively, owing to unconscious assumptions and habits built up in the course of learning, has been shown by Abercrombie and others; reception of information, recollections, observations and description, judgements or inferences are alike affected. These assumptions operate even with relatively simple material in visual illustions, in giving verbal definitions, or in understanding the meaning of a word, as well as in tasks for which more training is needed, such as interpreting X-rays. Teachers have various methods of combating this problem but it is questionable whether they are fully aware of its extent. They recognise that for the student to be led to new skills for which his existing habits and skills are inadequate they must organise new material in a way which is meaningful to him. But if the step is too great for him, or a problem too difficult, they tend to repeat their first explanation or to show again the steps of a solution to the problem without examining the student's assumptions and preconceptions. To do so involves either prior study of all possible wrong assumptions, with questions or procedures to correct them (as provided in some branching programmed texts) or discussion.

Johnson-Abercrombie experimented with undirected group discussions. Her aim was to avoid instruction in a 'correct' method but to develop a scientific method by stimulating students to work out problems among themselves through mutual questioning and correction. For example, in an early study with James and Venning, one group of students was trained to be observant in studying X-rays and other visual material by criticism of their own descriptions and inferences, so becoming aware of assumptions and preconceptions which influenced the receipt of visual information (James et al, 1956). It should be noted that the experimenter did not play the part of a director of discussion but was an onlooker who asked a question, or commented, somewhat in the manner of a psychiatrist in a group therapy session. The responses of the participants are also reminiscent of volunteers or patients in group therapy. Some inquired the purpose of it all and asserted that they had gained nothing from such undirected work (rejecting the experience), while others developed feelings of insecurity or hostility which they worked through; and nearly all were astonished, or even dismayed, on discovering how greatly unconscious assumptions had influenced their judgements. In subsequent comparison of this group with one conventionally taught, in observations of three X-rays, the trained group were superior to a highly significant degree; they made fewer false inferences, fewer inferences unaccompanied by descriptions, more of them considered two hypotheses rather than one only, and a smaller number were inappropriately biased by one test in dealing with the succeeding one. Evidently a change in behaviour did occur due to this kind of general discussion. Barnett (1958) used group discussion in a similar fashion with eight students using alternate two-hour meetings in a series of 24, for free discussion following the reading of a brief, and sometimes controversial, passage or article; like Abercombie, he observed the discussions without intervening until the end. He found that students came gradually to stick more to the point and to criticise each others' arguments more effectively — there was rather less arbitrary statement of personal prejudices and rather more attempt at rational argument, but these trends were only beginning to appear towards the end of 12 periods of discussion. Behaviour of some members of the group was noticeably influenced, eg in talking more, or less, or in becoming less aggressive.

What evidence there is suggests that lectures do not exert a comparable influence on students to make them think more critically. We have already mentioned the findings of Bligh, and of Houston and Pilliner. Elton (1965) compared students following courses of logic instruction and applied psychology, in their capacity to reason, as measured by Valentine's Reasoning Test, before and after their courses. Although the philosophy class studied a 16 week course devoted to the logical principles underlying valid thought, they made no greater improvement in scores than did the students of psychology. A promising line of investigation is suggested by Garbutt (1963) who collected text book definitions of terms used in accountancy. There were ten distinct definitions of 'capital'. When students were asked to define words commonly used in their first term's study many poor definitions, or none, were given for some of them, 'capital' proving the most difficult. It seems probable that, in a number of subjects, students cannot be intelligently critical because they simply do not know what they are talking about.

In surveying barriers to progress among students of social psychology. Gibson (1970) lists six main kinds of error: first, the notion that theories and hypotheses have been falsified when they have been shown not to apply in certain circumstances; second, over-generalisation of experimental results; third, failure to recognise particular experiments as building blocks in a wider theory, so that when experimental results cannot immediately be extrapolated to society at large, they are regarded as useless; fourth, lack of knowledge of research which would give precise meaning to terms such as 'balance', 'attitude', or 'prejudice'; fifth, rejection, complete or partial, of quantitative data, in the belief that essential aspects of the subject must be missed if quantitative data are insisted on; and sixth, confusion over what constitutes evidence. Thus he cites, in more detail, the kinds of complaints made by Abercrombie of biology students in the 1950s. The evidence, to date at least, is that her remedy may be the most effective.

Researchers in American also suggest that discussion plays an important part in the development of critical thinking (McKeachie, 1966). It is of interest, too, that the extensive and careful observations and experiments made by Inhelder and Piaget into the development of children's thinking have led to similar conclusions (Inhelder and Piaget, 1958). Piaget believes that the final stage, normally achieved in adolescence, in which children learn to accept

assumptions and hypotheses from which they make deductions, develops
primarily as a result of appreciating different viewpoints in discussion and
during co-operation. Indeed, in the absence of co-operation and the resulting discussion, he believes that this final level of thinking fails to develop
for, he says:

> "the coercions of other people would not be enough to engender a
> logic in the child's mind, even if the truths that they imposed were
> rational in content; repeating correct ideas, even if one believes
> that they originate from oneself, is not the same as reasoning
> correctly. On the contrary, in order to teach others to reason
> logically it is indispensable that there should be established between
> them and oneself those simultaneous relationships of differentiation
> and reciprocity which characterise the co-ordination of viewpoints."

Since the majority of students do not always reason logically there appears to
be sufficient evidence here for extensive use of discussion between students
or, as nearly as possible on a basis of equality, between teacher and students.

b.   Making diagnoses or decisions and solving familiar problems

Despite the importance of problem-solving and decision-making in university
work there is no systematic body of inquiry into processes of learning these
skills nor, until recently, any analysis of them with a view to more effective
teaching. But analysis of subject matter by teachers and psychologists
engaged in writing programmed books, or programmes for teaching machines,
and that by psychologists preparing 'flow-charts' of instructions enabling the
reader to arrive at decisions by means of simple alternative choices, have
indicated new approaches in teaching.

Gane, Horabin, and Lewis (1966) have begun work on clarifying decision-
making in industry and in government directives to the public, but they have
also suggested application in other topics including the making of diagnoses in
medicine. They give an example for the diagnosis of Reynaud's Disease and
Secondary Reynaud's Phenomenon, too complex to reproduce here, but a
simpler application to a legal procedure (Ross, 1975) suffices to demonstrate
the method although it does not require the cross-linking and diversity of
possible solutions of the medical diagnosis chart (Fig.1, p.71).

By this technique, everything which must be taken into account is itemised.
Methods of presenting the data can avoid production of excessively large
charts, either by listing instructions or by presenting a number of sub-charts.
The use of charts of these kinds in industry has resulted in dramatic improvements in training time and in general efficiency. Their value in university
teaching has not yet been explored, but the authors suggest that medical diagnosis charts may be used to update experienced practitioners with new developments or as useful 'memory-joggers'. They have an obvious value to the
advanced student in giving him, almost at one glance, all the factors which

FIGURE 1: Part of an algorithm prepared by Ross (1975)

PROCEDURES IN APPLYING FOR GRANTS

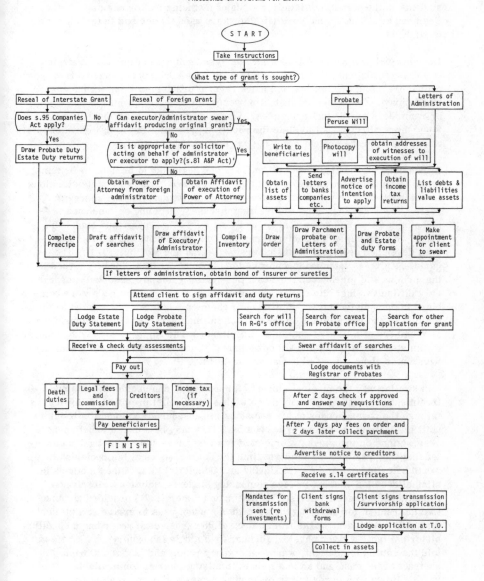

need to be taken into account in coming to a decision. The authors comment that the same advantages would hold if the chart dealt with completely different kinds of subject matter, such as technological information or the laws relating to taxation. Almost certainly, somewhat similar charts would guide students in the solution of familiar kinds of mathematical problems. Crombag et al (1972) and Ross (1972-6) have used the method in teaching law to students.

Designers of programmed books have analysed subject matter and strategies in solving problems to present them in such a way that specific methods of problem-solving are learned and more general problem-solving techniques are derived. One essential factor in successful solution appears to be recall, or reminder, of relevant principles. Where a reminder is needed it has been found more effective not to state the required principles but to ask questions which result in the student recalling or rediscovering them.

A technique increasingly used in America and beginning to be used in Britain is the 'simulation technique'. Tests or 'games' are used to simulate situations in which it would be unsafe or impracticable for students to take charge in reality, such as diagnosing and treating diseases, deciding on land uses, re-planning a town, and so on (Taylor and Carter, 1967; Taylor and Maddison, (1968). For example a structural game for undergraduate engineers has been developed at Heriot-Watt University (Cowan and Morton, 1973). The game, MOCO, is intended to improve the players' ability to identify forces in the members of pin-headed trusses. Substantial gains are reported except in very difficult items. Role-play, simulations, and project methods were combined in one polytechnical department of chemical engineering, when students were assigned roles either on the staff of an imaginery industrial company or as members of a firm of chemical consultants. The company's 'Works Manager' formulated the problem and the consultants' 'Capital Director' held discussions with teams about proposed industrial projects.

In a similar way the medical student, for example, can decide on tests and treatments, selecting as many as he wishes from a list provided, following through the consequences of his decisions in subsequent sections of a booklet until his 'patient' recovers or succumbs. This may be a useful supplement to observations on the wards. Some students who have used the method commented that they realised for the first time the consequences of the decisions they would be called on to make (McCarthy and Gonella, 1967). Other methods in clinical decision-making involve comparing students' solutions with those of consultants. A method devised by Helfer and Slater (1971) provided an objective instrument for assaying the process a student uses to arrive at a clinical diagnosis. A student works from a deck of 96 cards, each recording a specific historical fact, a given physical finding, or a single laboratory result. He is told the setting (outpatient, ward, emergency room) and is given a brief abstract of the case and an index sheet itemising information available on the cards. He selects cards in any order he chooses and compares his solution with those of five pediatricians by using a computer, so supplying detailed information as to his performance. A less mechanised approach for the general practice trainees involved comparing their diagnoses with those of a large group of principals (Richardson and Howie, 1972). A 'before' and 'after' study of antibiotic prescriptions suggested that this had been a useful experience. An inclusive investigation (Meals, 1973) consisted of a study of treatments by different consultants; but this seems to have attempted the skill of diagnosis merely by instruction, instead of involving students in making and correcting their own decisions, as learning theory may seem to recommend.

A book by British authors (Armstrong and Taylor, 1970) describes instructional simulation systems for use in higher education in military studies, management training, teaching of industrial relations, urban and regional studies, international relations, local government, and for development of social skills. Although their effectiveness is discussed, systematic evaluation of these methods has not been undertaken; they are used and valued because they partly supplied the need to study consequences of alternative courses of action and interaction between groups having conflicting feelings. As part of a university programme in careers guidance, simulation techniques were used during a five-day course on 'Information and Management' to give undergraduates a realistic idea of the work involved in this field (Graddon et al, 1974). Students' attitudes to the course were favourable. Similarly a game to teach skills in business studies is described by Hargreaves (1970). Snadden and Runquist (1975) have described the use of a programmable calculator to simulate experimental conditions in chemistry. Students are required to take laboratory decisions without conducting a full experiment. This means that, while the students learn fewer manipulative skills, they are more likely to be able to study a wide range of experimental conditions.

Simulation techniques have also been applied in teacher training by Tansey (1969) who provided case studies requiring decisions by 'teachers'. He points out the advantages of involving students in situations without risk which sensitise them to the real world of teaching and which bring together the theory and practice of education. Cruikshank (1963) has developed a teacher training scheme which can present the student with up to 31 different simulated problems related to teaching. This also forges close links between theory and practice.

Bligh (1972b) describes a method of teaching decision-making for teachers in training which combines group discussion with lectures or reading. They learn to consider a wide range of possible actions before taking a decision. But Bligh concludes that small leaderless groups seem to have an important role in teacher education and may at present be under-used.

c.   Solving unfamiliar problems; creative thinking

Ability to solve unfamiliar problems is becoming increasingly important in
scientific work, but there has been little systematic study of this skill. A new
line of inquiry into students' and lecturers' abilities and personalities
promises to cast more light on creativity in different fields. Hudson (1966)
has distinguished what he terms 'convergent' from 'divergent' thinkers: the
former excel in intelligence tests but tend to avoid ambiguity and prefer tests
with a single right answer; the latter are comparatively poor in standard
tests of intelligence but show great fluency in producing ideas. For example,
when asked to think of uses for a brick or a paper clip, the converger mentions one or two uses for each, whereas the diverger produces a large number.
'Divergence' and reasoning, as required in intelligence tests, appear to be
fairly unrelated. In addition to individuals biased in either direction, there
are 'high all-rounders' who score above the median in both directions, and
'low-all-rounders' who score below it in both (Joyce and Hudson, 1968).
Those with a bias tend to specialise in different fields: the able convergent
thinker chooses physical sciences, the outstanding diverger prefers the arts
or administration.

The qualities Hudson finds characteristic of original thinkers of either kind
are dedication to work, self-confidence, aggressiveness, a desire to go down
in history and a taste for taking risks. Creative workers describe themselves
as: inventive, determined, independent, individualistic, enthusiastic, and
industrious; whereas the non-creative select such adjectives as: responsible,
sincere, reliable, dependable, clear thinking, tolerant, and understanding.

A study by Connor of students' problem-solving identified several stages in
solving moderately familiar problems; but the students proved very poor at
unfamiliar tasks and it was rare for them to check on the adequacy or appropriateness of their conclusions (Connor, 1967). There seems to be a fairly
prevalent belief that inventive and creative workers are born, not made,
despite evidence that some university departments and certain teachers have
produced an unexpectedly high number of creative workers. There is evidence
too that the greater proportions of distinguished scientific workers in America
came from the East Coast initially but subsequently have been produced by
schools further and further West. Another American study suggests that
creativity is related to paternal absence or maternal dominance in childhood.

These findings suggest that creative talent could be a product of inborn ability
combined with favourable early experience, but that teaching at university
level can also be influential. For example creativity frequently results from
cross-fertilisation of ideas. In one department of chemistry each student,
in a group of four or five under the guidance of a tutor, is given a different but
related experiment. Cross-fertilisation of ideas is generated by discussion
when the experiments are written up (Nuffield, 1973).

Since good success in first-degree courses does not necessarily indicate
capacity for original work, nor a poor degree inability to think creatively,
there is some evidence that existing first-degree examinations and courses
fail to give sufficient opportunity for students to solve unfamiliar problems
or to show originality. Hudson (1966) observed that in Cambridge University
there was no relation between degree class and subsequent academic honours:
fully a third of the future FRSs at Cambridge had gained a second or worse at
some time during their university careers and the proportion among future
DScs was over a half. In an investigation in the Geography Department at
Newcastle University, undergraduates who did well in traditional examinations
performed at least competently in research but those who excelled in
research projects did not necessarily perform well in examinations; less than
half of them gained examination marks as high as B+ (Whiteland, 1966).

In consequence there is a move in some departments to take account of dissertations or other original course-work for the final assessment. Although
ability to think creatively is increasingly required, no British investigation
into teaching methods to encourage it has been traced. Nevertheless there are
many innovations in teaching. In both pure and applied sciences research projects and open-ended experiments for undergraduates are becoming fairly
common.

d.   Projects and problems

In 1965, Jones reported the use of carefully chosen projects in organic chemistry with third year students. The subject was chosen at the end of the Autumn
Term; practical work was undertaken the following Spring and the paper produced at the end of the term contributed to the students' final assessments.
Students worked jointly on a project, or two or three students worked on related
projects. This experiment was considered so successful that it was to become
the standard third and fourth year course in practical organic chemistry. In
engineering, projects were already employed by the middle of the last decade
and a wide variety is now in use. About a quarter of the university engineering
departments which replied to a survey had a favourable attitude towards open-
ended learning activities such as projects (Lee and Carter, 1972). Allen (1968)
and Jeffries and Leech (1969) describe 'design and make' projects in which
students prepare a design to the customer's specification, within an agreed
budget and time. Coekin's students work in groups and cost the manufacture
of production circuitry (1970). A different kind of project leads students to
relate engineering studies with those in humanities and social sciences. A
popular topic at Imperial College in 1967 required specific recommendations
by the students of, for instance, a suitable product for an engineering firm to
manufacture in a named developing country (Beard, 1967a). A few students
are able to pursue such topics overseas during summer vacations (Goodlad,
1970).

In an electrical machine laboratory, students choose their own projects
(Holmes, 1969). At Heriot-Watt University two difference approaches are

used (Cowan et al, 1970). First year students have recently designed balsa-
wood cantilever frames to support a loading bar some distance from a plane
surface. They were fabricated to detailed drawings produced by groups in
engineering drawing classes, and were tested to destruction in specially prepared rigs in the CCTV studio, students being asked to predict their modes of
failure. These experiments aroused great enthusiasm which led in many
cases to further inquiries. During the second year students select a topic for
a project from a tentative list of suggestions and are expected to take charge
of its development, depending on their tutors for guidance only; there is
considerable display of enthusiasm, intelligence and initiative — provided
that staff do not direct too closely. It is of interest that assessments in projects show no correlation with examination results.

A number of physicists describe projects which provide undergraduate students
with opportunities to attempt unsolved problems and to study a subject in depth
(Black et al, 1968; Elton et al, 1970; Foulds et al, 1969; Wooding, 1968).
Wooding lists topics which have been found suitable and outlines the development of several in more detail. He and his colleagues have found that they
must not work out the project very far before the student tackles it, or else
he tends to be guided too closely by the demonstrators. Alternative topics are
available if a student proves to be attempting a problem which is too difficult
for him.

Black and his colleages (1968) found that their students contrasted a feeling of
'sorting things out and learning' from projects with one of 'knowing nothing'
as a result of cramming for finals in the rest of the course. Projects are also
being employed with notable success in mathematics (Hirst and Biggs, 1969)
and in medicine (Edwards, 1967; Hayes, 1964; Wright, E.A., 1968).
Cornwall (1975) describes some similar developments on the Continent. In
courses where undergraduates lack the incentive, or ability, to undertake
original work, and in arts subjects, dissertations are set which require
mainly collection, collation and appraisal of published material. These are
common in colleges of education and in some technical colleges, and are
increasingly set in university departments. Similar approaches are used in
social sciences. Collier (1966, 1969) uses syndicates of five or six postgraduate students who work at group assignments in educational sociology.
In addition to greater involvement and satisfaction, the method leads to more
cogent reporting and allows greater independence than do traditional lectures
with tutorials.

In colleges of art and education reporting to the NUS over half the students
were working on a dissertation, thesis, or project, but only about one in
eight of students in technical colleges and universities were doing so. The
figure was particularly low in the two universities where three-quarters of
the students were neither told about, nor involved in, their departmental
research. Yet it is usually assumed that the universities train the researchers
of the future.

The Society for Research into Higher Education has published a book on the use of projects in higher education (Adderley et al, 1975), and one issue of Education in Chemistry (March 1974) is almost entirely devoted to discussion of projects. Hanson and Simmons (1972) note their value in crossing traditional subject boundaries. In two articles Harding (1973a, b) discusses varieties and purposes of projects, and problems in their use and assessment. Teachers who hesitate to introduce projects often give as reasons that suitable topics and apparatus are difficult to supply or that assessment presents too serious a problem. They find, for example, that tutors supply widely differing amounts of help, that work in groups makes individual contributions difficult to assess, and that since students tackle different topics there seems to be no adequate basis for comparison. Whilst there is some truth in this, the growing volume of suggestions for suitable topics may soon obviate the first difficulty. The others present a challenge to improve methods of assessment, rather than an excuse for ignoring an important aspect of students' work. Physicists at Queen Mary College, for instance, use independent interviews to assess group projects and set at least three intermediate half-hour tests containing questions on principles and on the individual's are of contribution.

At Sussex (Hirst and Biggs, 1969) the mathematicians have devised a common form of assessment for projects under four headings:

A Exposition: mathematical accuracy, clarity, literary presentation;

B Literature: understanding, relating different sources, finding new sources;

C Originality: examples cited, examples constructed, new treatments and proofs of standard results, simple generalisations, original researches;

D Scope of topic: conceptual difficulty, technical difficulty, relationship with previous studies, relevance of material included, coverage of the topic.

An extensive study of marking of A-level biology projects in which teachers and external moderators were given instructions about marking procedures resulted in satisfactory performance overall; but difficulties are discussed (Eggleston and Kelly, 1970). Handy and Johnstone (1974) have developed a method of testing performance in projects, involving an oral examination, which has proved very reliable, the uncertainty being of the order of 10 marks in 225. Of 4,000 projects which were completed and assessed during five years, only ten provoked substantial disagreements.

As one would expect, evidence suggests that opportunity to work creatively results in a greater output of creative work. Hayes (1964) investigated the effect of student dissertations as part of a graduate requirement in medical school. During the three years of the experiment, student participation in research increased: in 1961, 25 percent; in 1962, 26.5 percent; and in 1963, 45.5 percent of papers in the students' journal were based on original work. E.A. Wright (1968) also reports that an increasing number of students are publishing their work, mostly together with their supervisors, in the standard scientific journals.

Strategies in solving problems of in applying experimental methods require approaches which introduce students to a wide range of problems rather than intensive study of selected topics. Moreover, these problems should not be easy, for in this case no genuine problem-solving activity is involved. It is simply a matter of applying a well-known routine. In teaching problem-solving in pure mathematics at Oxford, about half the students attended problem-solving classes where very difficult problems were set, whilst the remaining half continued to attend tutorials (Hammersley, 1968). The performance of students who attended the classes became significantly superior to that of students having tutorials, and at all levels of ability. In applied mathematics classes where problems were relatively easy, no significant advances were achieved relative to the tutorial group. It seems likely that the stimulus of difficulty, together with the variety of attempts and discussion provoked, resulted in acquisition of a greater range of problem-solving skills.

In sciences, open-ended experiments are often set in addition, or in preference to traditional work in which expected results are known in advance. As in projects, this allows for a wide range in performance (Hughes and Morgan, 1970). At Melbourne, Lewis (1974) found little correlation between students' academic records and their skill in solving open-ended problems in engineering. Even in traditional experimental work it is possible to demand some independent thinking. Read (1969) insists that students should attempt to formulate and to test hypotheses to account for deviations they obtain from expected results. McDuffie (1973) reports that after initial puzzlement, when left to plan and write up experiments without class notes, sutdents show enjoyment. They also give attention to aspects of work such as calculations, and use of library resources, since they see the need for this.

The effect of continuous assessment of experimental work is said by Chalmers and Stark (1968) to be 'marked improvement and enthusiasm' and greater industry and enjoyment. It is assessed under three headings: accuracy, methodology, and comprehension, but since the course is designed to help students in these ways their increased enthusiasm may be due to better understanding rather than to continuous assessment as such. Martin and Lewis (1968) have attempted to clarify the purpose of experimental work for students by designing each experiment to achieve just one objective instead of the usual variety. They claim that this has resulted in considerable improvements in laboratory teaching.

In some cases whole courses have been altered so that experimental work can be relevant and challenging. The Nuffield inter-university biology teaching project (Dowdeswell, 1970) is developing methods which are largely self-instructional, but not costly. These will provide 'bridge courses', 'technique courses' (eg at Bath), aseptic techniques, and 'main courses' which are short courses that can be inserted anywhere, such as 'Enzymes'. In electrical engineering (Jenkins, 1968), in a new university, first year students receive sets of questions approximately every six weeks ranging from apparently simple to difficult, and are expected to answer as many as possible using any tools at their disposal. The solution may be theoretical, but if a student decides to carry out an experiment he must first of all design it, then select the equipment, carry out the work, and produce the results. The answers to all questions are written in a laboratory logbook, which is the only record of the student's work. Even more comprehensive changes have been undertaken at Heriot-Watt University (Cowan et al, 1970) where new methods are in use to direct students away from dependence on teachers to a student-centred process of genuine education. Learning sessions replace technological lectures and supporting tutorials. Objectives include development of skill in writing and reading, answering questions and solving problems, making observations and inquiries, and in writing reports of observations and deductions. Students make experiments of their own choice and open tutorials are used to deal with unanswered queries.

A survey of first year chemistry courses in Australia (Bryant and Hoare, 1970) shows that practical work in Queensland which 'teaches students to think for themselves' and 'produces data on which to build theory' scores the highest rating for interest.

In biochemistry in one of London's medical schools, students circulate round a number of experiments which each provide a surprise, generate a further question, or teach a technique which will be required later (Beard and Pole, 1971; Jepson, 1969). Students experiment on themselves or on each other or may have something to show at the end, such as a patient's enzyme pattern. Film loops showing use of experimental techniques are available for students to study when, and as often as, they please. Performance in the laboratory and in group discussion covering experiments both count towards final assessment. Students evidently enjoy this work but no evidence has been collected to show whether they learn more. Organisation of a large class to circulate among experiments is discussed here (Jepson, 1969). Other authors who consider this problem, arriving at a number of solutions, are Shouksmith (1969), and Jewell (1970).

CHAPTER 5: TEACHING FOR CHANGE OF ATTITUDES

I: ATTITUDES AND HIGHER ABILITIES

In discussion of methods of developing critical thinking we have seen that group discussion exposed prejudices and misconceptions, so changing attitudes as well as increasing capacity to think objectively. It is probable that certain attitudes preclude critical thinking or originality, whereas others promote them. The student who clings inflexibly to what he learned at an earlier stage, whether consciously or not, must remain uncritical, and any attitude which prevents him from experimenting, such as fear of being proved wrong or looking foolish, is likely to diminish his capacity for finding original solutions or making inventions. To be original it is essential to have an attitude favourable to novelty and exploration. Most probably the development of all higher mental skills is bound up with the concomitant development of favourable attitudes, but there is not enough evidence to show this conclusively.

We may reasonably expect increasing attempts to foster understanding of environmental influence on patients and clients in subjects such as medicine, dentistry, and law. Some medical schools have already set up departments of social medicine or epidemiology. Davies (1967) suggests that student dentists should "study the patient and the economic, social and political characteristics of the environment in which he lives", and points out "that in many ways the success of a dentist depends as much on understanding his patients as persons as upon his technical knowledge and facility". Students of law also have begun to study sociology. However, Levine and Bonito (1974) find that increasing exposure of students in their clinical years to faculty members who are involved in the kind of professional activities to which the students aspire may be a significant factor in the formation of students' attitudes, and consequently a barrier to change.

Such evidence as there is points to group discussion as a more potent method for changing attitudes than lectures or seminars conducted by tutors. A number of research workers have remarked on changes in attitude occurring in group members. Barnett (1958), for example, refers not only to increase in critical thinking but also to an influence on the behaviour of some members in becoming less aggressive. Hallworth (1957) used interpretations of group reactions to make members of a group of teachers more aware of processes influencing them, such as aggressive feelings towards authority, and so enabled them to become more self-critical and to develop skills concerned with group management.

For many years group discussion has been a method favoured for training in management. Smith (1969a, b) outlines the work in group dynamics known as 'T-groups'. As a result of their use, both he (1964, 1969b) and Cureton (1968) report increases in flexible attitudes and of more considerate behaviour,

ie of friendliness and sympathy towards others; but groups prove to be differently affected in these respects (Smith and Pollack, 1968). Similar favourable changes in attitudes were noted by Elliott (1958) among engineering
employees who took part in T-groups. Changes in actual behaviour were
investigated by Moscow (1968) who found greater tolerance, more skill in
action, and better understanding of others and of group interactions, among
those who had attended T-groups than among their colleagues who had not.

Smith identifies three kinds of social influence operating in groups toward
the leader: 'compliance' with some kind of pressure including response to
reward; 'identification' with the leader because his personality is attractive;
and 'internalisation', which occurs when influence is accepted from a leader
who is regarded as a trustworthy authority. In a study of 31 groups, Smith
(1969 b) found that high identification was not associated with favourable
changes in behaviour but resulted in an increase of assertiveness, or dominance, on the part of group members so influenced. Cooper (1968) showed
that a substantial positive correlation existed between verified change in
subsequent behaviour and group members' perception of the trainer as
'genuine' rather than as masking his true feelings. It is of interest that the
factors investigated in considering the leader's effect on the group are
relatively unconscious ones. Undoubtedly these are of consequence; but it
is commonly believed in universities that students' ability to modify and,
more important, to continue to modify their behaviour is more effectively
influenced by intellectual factors, such as insights into their own assumptions
or expectations through gaining a better understanding of human relationships
or from intellectual acceptance of a value. A tutor's knowledge of group
members' management problems seems likely, therefore, to be at least
equal in importance to his influence through personal qualities; but this has
not been studied.

In discussing acquisition of attitudes we should not forget the simple provision
of opportunities for students to display affective attributes such as critical
judgement and objectivity. Nay and Crocker (1970) have identified a large
number of attitudes which science students should be expected to acquire, and
suggest that they should constitute the basis for curriculum planning.

We may expect that experience outside academic institutions will modify attitudes; though some studies suggest that the direction of change is not always
in the direction desired by teachers. This could raise critical questions about
teachers and courses. As in the study by Morrison and McIntyre (1967), in
which increasing tender-mindedness of student-teachers during training was
reversed during their first year of teaching, so Preece and Flood Page (1974)
found a reversal of personality characteristics of sandwich-students during
their industrial training period. The clarity of course objectives and the
enthusiasm of both students and their university teachers were perceived less
favourably throughout the course. An evaluation of study abroad by Marion
(1974) did not find that students became more international, liberal, and self-
confident in their attitudes; but they were more realistic and consequently less
favourable towards the host country than before their visit.

From reports by individual teachers it is evident that 'games' involving role-playing influence attitudes by increasing insight into other people's problems. In one college of art, students playing the role of administrative staff developed sympathy towards an unpopular member of staff, realising that he was at the end of a communication line, and while he received many complaints he had no-one to consult or to pass them on to. Similar 'games' have been found helpful with managers in industry, while Ashley (1968) reports role-playing recorded on video-tape as an aid to social workers in understanding group interactions and thus to handling human relationships in general.

However, it is possible to use methods which influence attitudes without fostering criticism or insight. In an experiment by King and Janis (1956), students were asked to read a passage, either silently or aloud, advocating extension of the period of military service or, alternatively, to prepare a talk based on the arguments in the passage. Although oral reading gave students the greatest satisfaction, as indicated by their self-ratings, the improvised talks resulted in the speakers accepting the message in the persuasive communication significantly more often than those who merely read it. This seems to be a further example of more efficient 'learning' due to active involvement on the part of the learner. Nevertheless, few teachers would approve this as a method of 'teaching' unless it was used to make students aware that they could be so influenced. The result of this experiment suggests also that choice of textbooks and written exercises, and the unconscious biases of tutors in work they set, may have a more potent influence on students' attitudes than might have been supposed.

An aspect of influence on attitudes that has not been investigated in British universities is imitation of teachers, or identification with them, by students. There seems to be no doubt that this happens to some extent and it may be partly inability to learn in this way which accounts for antipathy to large classes or complaints by students of lack of contact with staff. Abercrombie (1965) quotes experiments showing the importance of perceived proximity of children to parent figures or teachers and the need for a feeling that authorities are approachable among adults. She comments: "This feeling of easy access is very important in all sorts of teaching situations, and we can encourage the accessibility or discourage it with minor adjustments of the environment". However, until investigations are made there are no findings to pass on to teachers who find it difficult to make themselves seem accessible.

II: MOTIVATION

An important objective of teachers is to increase the interest, or motivation, of the majority of students. We have already mentioned some of the factors which contribute to promoting them: clear definition of goals with inter-mediate and immediate objectives; prompt feedback as to success; active rather than passive, method of learning; and variety in teaching methods.

In addition, open-ended problems, dissertations, or 'research' projects can arouse considerable enthusiasm. Leininger (1975) reports on three motivational innovations in an engineering course involving slide projection, analysis of case studies, and role play.

In an experiment by Cullen (1974) two groups of students were given an intentionally dull lecture. The experimental group, asked to listen "as if they were 'A' students", scored higher on a short multiple choice test immediately after the lecture. Cullen's interpretation of this finding is that when students identify with a social group there are powerful motivational forces which can be harnessed for academic benefit. Presumably the converse is also true: if students are told they are incompetent they will perform less well.

An experiment which suggests new possibilities of increasing the motivation of students by personally-matched courses has been made by Joyce and Hudson (1968). It suggests that teachers and students resembling each other with respect to being 'convergent' or 'divergent' types form the most successful combinations in teaching. Perhaps this has some bearing on a peripheral finding in a study by Lewis and Pask (1964) of communication by mechanical means without verbal interchange. They reported that persons with high IQ were rather bad at communicating, partly because they overrated the receivers abilities but also because they were more vulnerable to the introduction of misinformation. This looks like the intolerance of convergers to ambiguity. It may be that, in teaching, convergers tend to give a lucid and logically presented account of subject matter, which is acceptable to student convergers, whereas divergent teachers favour digression which sparks off ideas in other divergers but frustrates the convergers' need for good organisation. In some cases, however, the relationship is more complex and teachers consistently gain a similar degree of success with the same sub-categories of students from one year to another.

CHAPTER 6: EVALUATION OF STUDENTS, TEACHERS, AND TEACHING
METHODS

I: METHODS OF ASSESSMENT AND TEACHING

Since one of the chief objectives of students in entering university is to obtain
a qualification, the form of assessment employed has a considerable influence
on emphases in content and methods of study. The effectiveness of teaching
and of teaching methods is therefore influenced by the ways in which students
are assessed.

In the past the only universal evaluation technique was the terminal, or final,
examination which was used to rank students and to determine whether they
had attained an 'agreed standard'. Numerous inquiries during the last 30
years or so have shown how ineffectively traditional exams, employing essay
questions, orals, and practical tests, achieved these objectives (Beard, 1969;
Cox, 1967). There is a demand today for more varied types of assessment to
meet the variety of aims in teaching, as well as for more evaluation of learning and teaching during courses. Black reports of an inquiry into university
examinations in physics (1968): "In general, departments replied that they
had not formulated rules about the style of questions, did not analyse
systematically the abilities tested by the questions, did not ask for model
answers, and did not ask for a marking scheme". There were no multiple
choice examinations, the questions being of the bookwork/essay type, or in
two parts — bookwork followed by a problem. All the questions were of the
same style, different papers testing different topics but not different types of
ability.

Similar limitations have been found in studies of chemistry examinations and
of examinations in biochemistry (Beard and Pole, 1971). But, in the latter
case, some papers allow, or require, a wider range of cognitive skills. In
one medical school a new type of examination for the second MB has been
devised in four parts: a multiple choice paper to test factual knowledge or
simple problems; a long essay for which six weeks preparation is allowed do
that students are encouraged to seek information for themselves and to think
originally; a paper of five traditional essay questions; and a paper requiring
students to evaluate experimental data in response to the question: 'Explain
as fully as you can what you consider is happening and try to account for all
the results recorded. Give some brief theoretical background against which
the problem and your solution can be set. Indicate what further investigation
would help test correctness of your explanation'.

Despite the findings of these investigations, a substantial number of teachers
are relatively uncritical of traditional types of examinations. In a study
among microbiologists in the United Kingdom and Ireland, essay-type
questions and orals were found to be almost universal and practical examinations were used by just over half. It was generally felt that term-time

assessment of practicals would be more satisfactory, but teachers wished to keep the existing form of examination in theory (Stewart-Tull, 1970).

A different pattern of examining in physics is reported by Elton (1968). At Surrey the final assessment is based on: (1) examinations at the end of the sixth and the beginning of the ninth terms, which each carry about a third of the marks; and (2) course work assessments, under five headings: (a) an essay written in the first summer vacation; (b) an open-book oral examination at the end of the fifth term; (c) full reports on three experiments selected by the examiners from those in the laboratory during the second year; (d) an oral examination on two other experiments, 30 minutes notice being given as to which ones; and (e) a project which is undertaken during the whole of the final term. Account is also taken of the level of the courses chosen during the first two years. Elton comments that although the reliability of marks for course-work is low, the validity is high.

A development towards greater diversity in examining in the arts is described by Brockbank (1969). Staff of the English department at York have retained the three-hour paper to test alacrity, rapid command of material and good recall, but they have introduced a variety of other forms of assessment. These include a 14 day paper limited to 1, 200 words, to encourage refinement of thinking and expression and a keen sense of relevance. Five tutorial essays are also submitted at the end of term for formal assessment, following rewriting after discussion with the tutor. Students may choose to be assessed in oral work in delivering, defending, and discussing a paper. In addition, long essays of seven to ten thousand words are assessed, some subsequent to tutorial guidance and others withouth, and an ancillary viva may be used in conjunction with any written form of assessment. It is of interest that about two-thirds of the students achieve comparable grades by any method, one-sixth each do better in papers written at leisure or in traditional papers, while one-tenth of these do either better or worse than by continuous assessment.

In medicine multiple choice tests are in fairly common use in terminal assessments and in some final examinations (Beard, 1967b). Anderson (1967) advocates in-course testing to motivate students to achieve their maximum performance. He points out the need to devise tests of clinical skills and habits that the students has acquired in relation to history-taking, clinical examination of the patient, bedside tests, etc, and suggests the use of microphones to aid assessment of the students' abilities in taking histories. The Todd Report also recommends the use of continuous assessment in clinical courses (Royal Commission on Medical Education, 1968).

The influence of methods of assessment on the effectiveness of teaching and teaching methods varies also with students' attitudes, personality traits, and aims. Walton and Drewery (1967) found that of those who did badly in an objective test in psychiatry the majority were highly extroverted; they were no good at medical examinations in general, not so good clinically, were prone to express value judgements to patients and to give advice, and were inclined at the beginning of the course to consider psychiatry irrelevant to their future professional work. Low scorers expressed disappointment with the amount and quality of teaching about drugs and physical treatments, whereas high scorers wished for more teaching in psychology and sociology. Patient management problems, already described in discussing decision-making skills, also make use of multiple choice questions. Palva (1974) describes a simple and cheap modification of these simulation tests.

At the University of Dundee, Knox (1971) has developed a modified essay (MEQ) based on procedures devised by the Royal College of General Practitioners (1971). The technique is in effect a serially-structured essay in which responses at each stage are relatively free, and consists in outline of a case study requiring the student to outline reasons for diagnoses, methods of patient management, considerations prior to taking action, information needed, etc. A marking schedule enables the student to score his own performance. Malleson (1967) also found that, in the case of clinical students, high drive introverts did best and low drive extroverts were the least successful, whereas in the second MB there was no different between these groups. He suggested that the second MB course was so highly structured and controlled that there was little latitude for the individual's personality to influence his attainment.

Other researchers have also shown the superiority of introverts as examinees. Davies and Mowbray (1968) found that students with high introversion scores had a very significantly higher mark in psychiatry. The Entwistles (1970), who explored the relationship between personality, study methods, and academic performance, report that introverted first year students had a better academic record, slightly better study methods (ie they worked more carefully), thought ahead, were conscientious, and recognised the importance of working conditions. In a second study, with Wilson (1971), performance proved to be strongly related to study methods, motivation, and introversion scores, but had no relation to emotional stability. A study-methods scale distinguished between the worst students and the best, and the extroversion score between the best and the remainder. They recommend questionnaires on motivation and study methods as a means of detecting potential failures for remedial action. Differences between introverts and extroverts have prompted other inquiries. Leith and Wisdom (1970) found that introverts did better with more structured methods whereas extroverts fared better with less structured ones. Trown (1970) showed in a number of studies that among children introverts were superior in performance when rules were presented before examples, whereas extroverts were superior when examples were presented first. This held good for immediate learning, retention, and transfer of learning to similar situations. In addition, it held good for different levels of both intelligence and anxiety. Thus the common finding that introverts do better in university courses may be as much a reflection on the courses and examinations as on the students.

A fairly new approach to evaluation in the UK is to invite students to evaluate their own performance. In a study of its effects, Kennel, Tempio, and Wile (1973) found that when students initiated discussion of their problems and weaknesses they were usually amenable to the tutors' suggestions and plans for assistance. This contrasted with the arguments, objections, and defensiveness that often followed even mild criticism in tutor-directed evaluation conferences. Most students considered that the approach was worthwhile and that it influenced their subsequent behaviour.

Assessment of course work has not yet been studied in any detail. Commonly-used methods such as exercises, essays, problems, etc, which are marked some time after the student completes the work, are being increasingly criticised because they often fail to detect causes of students' difficulties, tend to be marked uninformatively, and provide corrections, if any, too late to influence learning at the critical time. Three new types of evaluation are being developed to give more objective and immediate assessment both to teacher and student.

II: EVALUATION OF TEACHERS

The first attempts to evaluate university teaching concentrated on qualities of the teacher; yet this has doubtful logic. It only requires one unmeasured vitiating fault to annul the effectiveness of a teacher with one style — the effectiveness of another teacher with a different style may be unaffected by the same fault. Possibly these first attempts were inspired by a desire to reward the best teachers in university departments even if they were not outstanding research workers, for it is generally believed that it is excellence in research alone which gains advancement. Rating scales were devised in America and were later modified for use abroad. In Queensland, for example, students were invited to express their reactions to their teachers' perform-ances with a view to obtaining a group opinion from a set list of characteristics of teachers (Schonell et al, 1961 a and b). A teacher meeting with the students' approval might find that, in his case, students had underlined such statements as: 'knows subject thoroughly; interested in teaching; never stops learning; always well prepared; presents material in systematic fashion; uses varied methods; sets high standards; .....; has a sense of humour'; whereas for his less fortunate colleague they might endorse: 'Often does not know subject; is unsystematic, vague and rambling; has no clear standards; shows undesirable personal qualities such as laziness, impatience, prejudice, intol-erance; has annoying mannerisms; will not admit errors;....' But attempts to achieve group views in this way, which really had a bearing on teaching, were unsuccessful. Teachers perform differently when they teach different topics or classes of different abilities, or when they employ different teaching methods; they may even perform well in one university department and indifferently in another. Students, or colleagues, also differ in the way they assess teaching; some praise highly a conscientious teacher who covers the syllabus thoroughly in well-organised lectures, while others look for inspira-tion and originality, preferring to obtain basic information in private study.

Ratings of one particular teacher on 44 characteristics, on two occasions separated by two-and-a-half years, correlated significantly (0.71) (Foy, 1969). But although this suggests that students' assessments are fairly reliable, it cannot confirm their validity (indeed, Leyton (1966) suggests that students build stereotypes of their lecturers). Nor does it show that the students necessarily value the same things. Using the Osgood Semantic Differential and a variety of statistical techniques, Sherman and Blackburn (1974) concluded that dynamic, pragmatic, amicable and intellectually-competent teachers receive the highest ratings for teaching, but when other techniques are used other parameters may be important.

Gruneberg and Startup (1975) have suggested that first-year students have an inadequate knowledge of the lecturer's role, and that this ignorance should be remedied by an induction course. In response to a questionanire indicating the hours spent by lecturers in various activities, one-third of the students did not mention research and over 60 percent did not mention administration.

It is commonly accepted that university teachers have a conflict between the demands of teaching and research, yet there have been few studies of the motivation of academic staff. The work of Halsey and Trow (1971), which classified university teachers according to their teaching/research orientation, assumed the conflict in the way the questions were framed; but it is possible that one teacher could be more or less motivated towards both than another.

In one college, the most important reasons for conducting research, in descending order of importance, were: enjoyment, advancement of knowledge, promotion, prestige, duty, and financial reward. Eight-six percent felt under some pressure to publish and 26 percent felt great pressure. The pressure felt was inversely related to seniority (Startup and Gruneburg, 1976).

III: ASSESSMENT OF TEACHING

In more recent studies of teaching, therefore, it is the teaching itself which is assessed, either by testing how much information students have gained or by inquiring early in a course whether the teaching could be adjusted in any way to meet students' needs more fully. In some departments frequent testing is used for the information of staff and students. In the Department of Mechanical Engineering, University of Birmingham, weekly quizzes (brief written tests) are used in this way, a generally poor result being accepted as a reflection on teaching in that topic (Beard et al, 1964).

Inquiries into the effectiveness of a teacher's communication with his class cover a wider range of information. Students may be asked to endorse one of five statements about the amount of material during a period of teaching: 'far too much, ..., satisfactory, ... practically nothing worth saying'; or (of speed) 'spoken too fast, ..., about right, ... tediously slow' etc; as well as making comments on conditions in the room, use of audio-visual aids, value and quality of applications or examples, adequacy of answers to questions, and so on (Beard, 1967 b; McVey, 1967). In this way, even if the replies are somewhat damaging to the teacher's self-esteem, he has a guide to future action which should enable him to communicate better with that group of students.

For evaluation of teaching, Wragg (1970) used the Flanders' Interaction Technique. This involves allocating the teacher's and pupils' contributions to one of ten categories at regular short intervals, say every three seconds, eg: praises or encourages, asks questions, lectures or gives facts etc, students initiate talk, silence and confusion. To his surprise he found "an almost unbelievably stable pattern". Analysis of the first 35,000 tallies collected by students of education showed more than a third of the time given to 'lecturing', nearly a quarter to 'silence and confusion' and about an eighth each to teachers asking questions or to pupils' responses. Bligh (1971) describes a modification of this technique suitable for use in small-group teaching in higher education. Where the teacher plays a minor role (at least overtly) or where the emotive aspects of students' contributions are important — as in tutorials or 'free group discussion' — he recommends the use of Bales' Interaction Process Analysis which is described by Sprott in Human groups (1958, pp 130-132). Alternatively students may be invited to comment specifically on a method. Moss (1973) found that students in a computing science course commented more freely on the use of video-tape in teaching than they would normally do on a lecturer's performance.

As a more direct measure of the achievement of teaching objectives, Bligh (1974, 1975 a) has developed a 'Truth Functional Test' at eight cognitive levels. The test consists of statements to which students may respond 'agree', 'disagree', or 'don't know', and which bear a precise and specifiable logical relationship to statements used in teaching. This is quick to administer and to mark, is easier to construct than multiple-choice questions and encourages less guessing, and it may be modified for affective objectives or an infinite number of cognitive levels. It has in addition the unique feature of being objective both in setting and marking, and is suitable for use during a period of teaching to obtain prompt feedback.

Cantrell (1971) reports assessments of the lectures given by thirty visitors to a medical school. He used a rating scale considering: (1) methods, aids used, voice production and use; (2) response of the audience; (3) evidence of awareness of the audience on the part of the speaker; (4) structure of the lecture; (5) incentives to learn more; and (6) personality factors such as humour, enthusiasm, relaxation, and ability as an actor. His table of results suggests a bi-modal distribution of ability, correlated with seniority.

Johnson, Rhodes, and Rumery (1975) point out, however, that there is no generally-accepted way of either defining or assessing the acitvity of teaching. Most attempts, they say, are separated from the educational context, with its social and cultural reference; current approaches to evaluation lack adequate theoretical development and confuse measurement with evaluation.

IV: STUDENTS' OPINIONS OF TEACHING METHODS

Students' opinions of teaching methods have been inquired into on a number of occasions. The Hale and Robbins Reports (University Grants Committee, 1964; Committee on Higher Education, 1963) survey opinions of students in the majority of universities and colleges. Marris (1965) obtained views from students of three universities and one technical college. The NUS Report of 1969 (Saunders, 1969) gives views of students of two universities, two technical colleges, two art colleges and two colleges of education. Views of medical students were collected and published in 1965 and, a year later, students of the Royal Dental College published a report of their views on lecturing in the college. McLeish (1970) and Stones (1969) have inquired into the opinions of students in colleges of education. In addition, surveys of students' views have been made in Australia (Australian Vice-Chancellors' Committee, 1963; Schonell et al, 1962), by individuals in single colleges, and by research workers in the course of investigations into teaching methods.

In general there is considerable criticism of lectures. The Hale Report concludes: "The general tenor of the student memoranda is very similar. It is highly critical of the lecture. The principal desiderata are fewer and better lectures, closer staff-student relations, and more teaching by tutorial and seminar." In reply to the invitation to distinguish characteristics of good and bad lectures, 44 percent mentioned points of delivery such as audibility, speed of delivery, diction, and legibility of writing on the board, 43 percent commented on clarity and order, 36 percent stressed the importance of interest. Scientists, in particular, remarked on their need for ease in taking notes, nonscientists referred fairly frequently to the desirability of originality, and about 20 percent of all students emphasised that lectures should be comprehensible and should provide a guide to further study. Overall percentages obtained in Marris' inquiry were fairly similar, but, in addition, about 20 percent of students felt a need for more guidance.

Despite their stringent criticisms of lecturing, when asked what changes they would propose only $12\frac{1}{2}$ percent in Oxbridge and 20 percent in London (with intermediate proportions in other universities) suggested fewer lectures. One may conclude, perhaps, that it is lecturing technique rather than the method itself which is criticised. In the unofficial surveys made for the report, 65 percent of all students who replied wished for no change in the proportion of lectures, 14 percent expressed a wish for fewer lectures, but 10 percent would have welcomed more. On the other hand, when asked similar questions about tutorials and seminars, the vast majority of those already having some wished for more; in Sheffield, for example, 73 percent wanted more while merely 4 percent wished for fewer. Only in Cambridge where tutorials are more frequent was there substantially less desire for an increase in their number.

The NUS report of 1969 (Saunders et al, 1969) gives average hours per week spent in formal lectures in the pairs of colleges investigated as: 4 (art college), 14 (education), $12\frac{1}{2}$ (technical), and 8 (universities), but the students from art colleges spent 30 hours per week in studio work. Preferences they stated suggest that the university students were content, but that those having more lectures would have liked fewer; education 12, technical 10; but art students would have welcomed five hours instead of four. In these eight colleges, three hours per week was the typical period spent in seminars — except in the college of art (one hour) — and less than two hours were spent in tutorials except in the technical college (three hours). Student teachers wished for six hours in seminars, but other students would have preferred about three hours each in seminars and tutorials. The average time students wished to spend in practicals and written work corresponded closely with the time they did spend.

When asked to rate teaching methods for effectiveness, 58 per cent of the students rated lectures as effective, but other types of teaching were more likely to be rated 'very effective', indicating a preference for smaller groups and personal teaching.

The Report on Medical Education by the British Medical Students' Association (1965) is a source of student opinion on teaching methods which is represent- ative of a large sample, although possibly not a statistically representative one. Students considered that, in general, they were given insufficient oppor- tunity to play an active part in their own education; they advocated a reduction in the number of lectures, but improvement in the standard of remaining ones, partly by increased use of such audio-visual aids as films, slides, charts and demonstrations. Methods advocated to increase students' participation were the Grand Tutorial and Corlab, in both of which students arrive already pre- pared for questioning or discussion. There was also considerable demand for more tutorials to cope with individual difficulties, and a request for more extensive use of the new media. These views are to some extent supported by recommendations in the Todd Report (1968) which advocates a considerable reduction in the number of lectures.

In 1969, Hawkins reviewed students' opinions on practical biochemistry in the London medical colleges. Two-thirds of the students enjoyed it 'a little' or 'not at all', and one-half felt that it was no help in understanding the subject. Just under half felt that substitution of demonstrations of modern apparatus and techniques for practical work would make the courses fully comprehensible, and more than four-fifths favoured additional tutorials. A majority preferred experimental work (if it continued) to consist of short experiments with an occasional long project.

A point on which opinions differed between Australian students and their teachers, and which is frequently raised in Britain also, is the provision of duplicated notes. Eighty-three percent of Australian students liked them because they found them closer to the course, more accurate than their own notes, and useful in revision (Australian Vice-Chancellor's Committee, 1963). In Britain, students more often mention the waste of time and hindrance to understanding which results from taking notes (Marris, 1965; Saunders, 1969). Australian teachers were divided, some regarding notes as spoon-feeding, an encouragement to 'swotting' from notes only and to passivity on the part of students; these pointed to the strain on secretarial resources and the consequent tendency to use the same notes from year to year. But no-one, it seems, objected to laboratory notes, field notes, or instructions for experimental work, or to bibliographies and essay or reading lists. Those who favoured the use of duplicated notes considered that they saved time for the lecturer, allowed him to digress profitably without leading his students to lose sight of the central argument, compensated for lack of suitable books or for library deficiencies, and might incorporate journal material that was not readily accessible. The inquiry showed that the kind of notes provided differed widely, from brief outlines provided in advance, or occasional summaries, to verbatim reports of most lectures or very full notes comprising hundreds of pages which served as the department's 'text-book'. It is the latter which is most generally disapproved of by students.

As we have already seen in an earlier section (Elton et al, 1970; MacManaway, 1970) there is now some evidence that duplicated notes can be highly effective when well designed and used to promote activity on the part of students. Students consulted for the NUS report regarded seminars as important for interchange of ideas, stimulus of creative thinking, and improvement of self-expression, but less suitable for consolidation of learning and study in depth. Common complaints were of 'domination by one or two students', dependence on staff, and bad and insufficient preparatory work by students. Most thought that ideally there should not be more than ten people participating and that the seminars should not last for more than one hour. In a survey of more than one thousand college-of-education students by Stones (1969), over half preferred seminars to lectures and tutorials, rating them highest for developing standards of judgement, inspiring ideas, learning to present an argument, discussion of practical work, and revision. Tutorials were considered most useful for obtaining feedback on progress, feeling known, and planning future work. In the NUS report over half the students thought the major functions of tutorials were to consult tutors on work or other matters and receive detailed criticism of prepared work, but opinion was evenly divided as to whether an academic tutor should be the same person who advised on personal problems. Over half thought that tutorial groups should meet once a week and should contain a maximum of three students.

However, not all students think alike. It is widely recognised by teachers that students vary in their preferences for teaching methods. This recognition is frequently coupled with a galaxy of dubious assumptions. For example, it is frequently assumed that these variations are related to personality factors and that the relationship is both linear and causal. Similarly it is often assumed that variations in students' preferences for different teaching methods are positively related to their learning from them. Consequently many studies have confined themselves to relatively simple relationships. In one college of education, Woodford (1969) found that, although on the whole students preferred methods encouraging participation, more intelligent and less stable students preferred restricted participation, whilst introverted students only slightly preferred these methods to more formal ones. In an investigation relating personality traits to attitudes to lectures, seminars, and tutorials, McLeish (1968) found eight roughly-distinguishable types. These ranged from 'enthusiasts' who liked all methods, to rebels who liked none. Others markedly favoured methods in which lectures played a major part, or those which emphasised student participation. The former of these two groups appeared to be tough-minded introverts with high security need, tending to be submissive and to favour formal methods and having high scholastic values. The latter valued new experience and freedom for themselves more strongly than other groups and were more anxious; they were also more radical in their educational views and more extroverted. In a later study (1970) in colleges of education he found lectures to be unpopular with independently-minded students and with those who believed that the educational system required substantial change; they were favoured by older, more conservative, stable, submissive, unsure or religious students. Those favouring lectures took a more favourable view of the staff, and the converse was also true.

Comparing students' attitudes to lectures, seminars, tutorials, television, and tests of semantic association, Palmer (1975a) found that students with 'activity' and 'potency' attitudes were more favourably disposed towards didactic methods, TV, and lectures, while those with 'evaluative' attitudes were more favourable to discussion. In a further inquiry by Palmer (1975b), introverts preferred television, and neurotic students disliked self-instructional techniques in practicals, while those with greatest ability were less inclined to want contact with the teacher when being shown demonstrations.

Students within one school or one discipline serve to show the diversity of responses. Joyce and Weatherall (1959) found that a sample of their students enjoyed discussions initiated by tape-recording more than seminars conducted by teachers; they returned singly, or in small groups, to listen again to the recordings more often than students attending seminars returned for further information or discussion. However, they considered seminars more useful than discussions. Lectures were considered by all groups to be outstandingly the most useful methods, and three-quarters of the students considered them most enjoyable. Reading was considered almost as useful as practicals but much less enjoyable. In this study the authors point out that an overall slight negative correlation between total estimates of usefulness and enjoyment, with final marks in three sections of the text, suggest that the more critical students performed better and the less critical less well. In an

earlier study (1957) there was negligible correlation between students'
impressions of their enjoyment of a method and success in corresponding
tests. They observed "It follows that performance and students' judgements
cannot both be criteria of the efficiency of teaching methods." On the other
hand, since different teaching methods tend to foster different intellectual
skills, the method of testing could favour one method unduly.

In an Australian study (Kitchen, 1969) external students experiencing a wide
range of teaching methods including tape-recordings, tutors' visits, correspondence, written assignments, lectures and 'vacation schools', rated the
methods on a variety of criteria. Students were generally satisfied with
teaching but a well-planned library proved to be most highly valued. Students
differed most in valuing different major means of study, in preferring teaching methods with informal and more personal kinds of teaching, and in
concern for spoken and oral aspects.

Familiarity with high standards of professional television might lead students
to be critical of the efforts of their teacher, but the reaction of radiologists
at Glasgow (Davidson and Thompson, 1970) was overwhelmingly favourable.
However, James (1970) found that although students preferred learning from
video-tape they were more successful when using an instruction booklet.
Students of psychiatry considered CCTV to be more effective than either
programmed instruction or the conventional case demonstration; and as
measured by a multiple choice test, the second judgement was correct, but
the first was incorrect.

To lead classroom technique, Neale (1967) used live demonstrations, relayed
television, recorded television, and a lecture, and found that students'
preference was in the order which reflected immediacy, or the reality of
experience.

It is of interest that there is so much to report about students' and teachers'
opinions of different teaching methods, but that there are still relatively few
inquiries into their effects on learning. Although consumer satisfaction
deserves some consideration, in the long run it is measures of effective
learning which count towards students' success and contribute most to improvements in teaching method.

V: ASSESSMENT OF COURSES

Along with the development of curriculum theory during the past ten years,
there has been a growing interest in evaluating entire courses. Feldman and
Newcomb (1973) have summarised vast quantities of American data on the
impacts of colleges on courses. Bernstein and others have emphasised the
ways in which courses classify knowledge and form academic boundaries.
For example, Baron (1975) has suggested three theories of the content of
courses: the 'Bundle of Knowledge' theory gives pieces of knowledge which

may be related and tested; the 'Developmental Stage' theory emphasises general growth and maturity; while the 'Component' theory emphasises skills which will be useful. Bruner, like many educationists before him (eg Whitehead), has stressed the difference between the content and process of courses. In this book we are not concerned with these types of assessment, but with assessments insofar as they reflect teaching methods used in courses.

One of the earliest attempts to assess entire courses was at the University of Bradford, where a longitudinal study of the educational and occupational values of the 1966 intake was set up by Musgrove. This has been continued mainly by Smithers, who has recently published a book on the subject (1976). Evaluation in these studies tends to take the form of seeking students' opinions, unlike the evaluation of systematically-designed courses having stated objectives, which tends to estimate or measure students' success in the courses or of changes in aspects of behaviour.

Following his earlier inquiries Musgrove (1969) noted that students of science and technology seemed to find university life more problematical than students of arts and social science, especially with regard to academic study. They more often admitted to finding lectures difficult, to feeling overwhelmed by academic work, and to being worried by the thought of examinations. However, he noted that their problems relating to academic skills were less widespread in 1968 than in 1966, and that students who had spent periods in industry more often found their university studies interesting and seemed to have gained in academic self-confidence.

Davie and Russell (1974) discuss findings concerning industrial courses in Australia. Analysis of examination results over a 9-year period shows a significant improvement after exposure to industrial experience, both by comparison with the previous performance and by comparison with equivalent full-time student performance. In this comparison the co-operative (sandwich-course) student is seen to gain in social and academic maturity and in technical preparedness for his role as a graduate. Smithers's findings (1976) are more mixed and cannot fairly be summarised in brief. Amongst them he notes that science students found industrial experience more congenial than did technology students, perhaps because they are given responsibility for a project. Students as a whole saw the main advantage of industrial experience in learning about people and how to get on with them, and in learning about firms.

At Edinburgh, Miller and Parlett (1974), in studying examination results in three departments of the University, have challenged the traditional approach to evaluation by measurement, advocating instead an exploratory approach. This is an attempt to comprehend the whole system of assessment rather than to answer a list of pre-determined questions. In order to do so they used techniques involving interviews, questionnaires, observation within the departments, or analysis of documents, redefining the problems and areas of inquiry as the study progressed. They see the chief function of such an inquiry as providing information and insight for professional educators.

Thus in their study of development in one department of a short answer
paper designed to test students' capacity to think rather than to memorise,
they follow progress from preliminary description of the new paper by three
members of staff, through discussion of it and contributions by other staff
members, a decision to make all questions compulsory followed by discovery
that some 'first-class' students were unable to answer very basic types of
question, to inquiry into the discriminating power of the paper, students'
reactions, and inter-marker consistency.

At the Open University, where an Educational Technology Unit of more than
30 members is continuously engaged in the largest evaluation project in
Britain, McIntosh (1974) discusses problems involved in evaluating multi-
media educational systems, noting that this cannot be confined to the 'test
and measurement' model. She suggests that evaluation cannot be tidy or
controllable, and that no one evaluative technique can be dominant;
research therefore plays only a part in the total evaluation. She sees evaluation as contributing to: (i) discovering whether there is a need for a course;
(ii) locating, defining and characterising the target group of the course;
(iii) pre-testing the course or its components; (iv) providing short-term
remedial feedback whilst the course is running; (v) determining whether or
not the course works in terms of the needs of the students and the needs of
course producers and conveyers; and (vi) determining whether or not the
objectives of the resource provided have been met. However, she notes problems in defining objectives adequately since different objectives are held by
various groups of people: society at large, a group devising the course, an
individual instructor, students 'users' of the course, potential employers,
and others affected by the student. Thus unexpected outcomes may be more
important than achievement of objectives. Bates (1974) has suggested that
course teams, as used in the Open University, could be a powerful medium
for innovation in other institutions.

Evaluation of systematically-designed individual courses based on defined
objectives normally has two aspects: measurement of students' achievements
of the objectives as compared with a control group; and inquiry into views
and opinions of teachers and students. A number of these studies has already
been mentioned (Brewer, 1974; Hearnshaw and Roach, 1974; Oosthoek and
Ackers, 1973; Sullivan, 1974; Witters and Kent, 1972; and Wyatt, 1975).
Blunt and Blizard (1973) found that such a course resulted in considerably
better examination results and that group discussion fostered more favourable
attitudes to anatomy. Leytham and James (1973) outlined and assessed
achievement of objectives in teaching by videotape; Hartley (1974 b) surveyed
programmed courses, including Keller variations, in psychology and their
evaluation; R.N. Smith (1971) assessed a programmed instructional test in
clinical pharmacology. Advantage of all such courses lie in the careful
preparation which they receive and the continuous assessment of students'
performance which enables teachers to make modifications in order to maintain or improve performance. Van der Klauw and Plomp (1974), on the basis
of experience and data received, present a scheme in which the main

characteristics of successful individualised study systems are outlined. However, Hoberoek (1971), and Gessner (1974), obtained contrasting results for courses in engineering.

Where less-structured courses are assessed it tends to be more difficult to say just why they succeed or fail. Gilliland and Gibbons (1971) used multiple choice tests to assess learning during short refresher courses for hospital doctors, medical students and research assistants. The doctors and students made significant gains on questions taught. Stansfield (1971) similarly tested doctors who attended lectures at a postgraduate centre. They too made significant gains if they had attended lectures in the subject tested, differences between attenders and non-attenders being greatest for those lectures that had been judged most successful. In a study using taped lectures, and questions on plant physiology for students to answer and to draw their own conclusions from, Marinos and Lucas (1971) found that students who had audio-visual aids consistently retained information better; but it is not clear how the assessment related to teaching methods or the teachers' aims.

Freeman and Byrne (1973) have reported on a succession of courses for new entrants to general practice at one of the now numerous postgraduate training centres. They devised tests to evaluate changes in knowledge, skills and attitudes on a pre-course and post-course basis. The first battery was given both to general practitioner trainees and to their general practitioner tutors; some social scientists were also tested. In tests of medical knowledge the two groups proved equally good, but the tutors exceeded the trainees in medical skills. In more general tests of ability, the GP trainees proved stronger diagnostically than verbally, and were far more articulate in oral than written verbal performance; the reverse held, in each case, for social scientists. In personality the trainee GPs were characteristically 'convergent' in their orientation but were well balanced on measures of introversion/extroversion.

Change in attitudes or expectations during courses has been the major concern of other investigators. Barraclough and Lippiett (1972) used a multiple choice test to assess gain in knowledge and a standardised scale to measure conjectured change of attitude by curates attending a psychiatry course. There was a significant gain in knowledge, but their attitudes which were initially favourable did not become significantly more so. Cox and Kontiainen (1974) compared attitudes of trained trainers, untrained trainers, and trainees, to teaching in general practice. They found that they could discriminate between these groups on two dimensions: on attitude on the part of GPs toward trainees as fellow colleagues and participants in practice vs viewing the student as an observer; and on a dimension contrasting process-orientation with product-orientation. Trained trainers moved towards seeing their role as involving more active teaching, but had not become so much like medical-school teachers as the trainees seemed to expect. In an earlier study (Kontiainen and Cox, 1973) trainers' attitudes changed on the whole in the directions viewed as desirable by course tutors. Sheldrake (1974) discusses at some length the diversity of expectations of medical students studying a behavioural sciences course and considers some of the factors contributing towards students' attitudes.

A course for freshmen engineers (Langholz and Sekay, 1975) seems too vaguely defined in its aims. It is therefore not surprising to find that an attempt to evaluate changes in students' orientations and motivations showed that it had little impact.

Many attempts to evaluate courses include, or are limited to, inquiries into 'consumer satisfaction'. In this respect medical schools in London had already made considerable progress in the late 1960s, for the majority of teachers replying to a questionnaire reported that they 'always' (25 percent), 'frequently' (25 percent) or 'sometimes' (27 percent) invited criticisms or suggestions from their students about courses or teaching (Beard, 1967b). Teachers in three dental schools probably corresponded more nearly with the majority of university teachers, the respective percentages being approximately 20, 16, and 28.

Student satisfaction with courses and teaching is negatively related to the amount of coercion their teachers use (Jamieson and Thomas, 1974). Yet coercion appears to be widespread at all educational levels and appears to be accepted and even expected. Reid-Smith (1969) attempted to measure student satisfaction with a course in librarianship taught chiefly by lectures, seminars, and syndicate method. Opposing opinions were recorded, but mature students were uniformly more appreciative. It was clear that students had not thought about the purpose of this course beyond aiming to get a qualification. Except for sessions spent in reporting back, syndicates were the most popular. Discussions in the local bar were more popular than those elsewhere.

In a postgraduate school where very item of a teaching programme was graded on a three-point scale, a fall was reported in the number of dissatisfied course members, staff were stimulated by knowing that they were assessed, and students co-operated more willingly (Gauvain, 1968). In the later report Gauvain (1970) concludes that the aims of a course should be made known to students. Students should be asked to state their aims in applying to attend, and course assessments by students should always be followed by discussion. In a further study, Gauvain, Brook, and Aldridge (1971) evaluated an experimental course in psychiatry for industrial medical officers by use of a questionnaire concerning the organisation of the course, its relevance, methods of teaching, and the aims of the course members. In addition an anonymous 'examination' was given to assess gain in knowledge of psychiatry and participants' ability to make diagnoses on medical and psychodynamic models or to consider a psychodynamic approach in more detail. On the whole, course aims seemed to be achieved and participants were satisfied.

An inquiry to medical students following a brief experience in general practice (Dean, 1971) showed that more than 90 percent of the students considered this experience valuable, and 57 percent thought more favourably of general practice as a result. About twice as many students having experience of general practice, compared with controls, selected it as first choice of career.

Students of engineering given the opportunity to comment on a design course (Holgate, 1971) rated the tie-in with theory and other subjects as rather unsatisfactory. They desired an introductory talk, in addition to notes, to help them get under way with the design exercise. Students also commented on an excess of formulae in notes, use of jargon, and excessive background material, and criticised marking in general.

The difficulty of satisfying all the students in a course of lectures is stressed by Falk (1967) who recorded comments by four students on the same series of lectures in history :-

(1)   'Made a fascinating period of history very flat.'

(2)   'Congratulations on an exceedingly workmanlike job of teaching as opposed to purely lecturing.'

(3)   'Gives students impression that they are back in the schoolroom. By this I mean over-simplification, over-clarification.'

(4)   'These lectures were the best I've had this year.'

It is true that the range of ability among first-year students in Australia is very wide, but even in England the opinions of teaching capacity of lecturers tends to vary from student to student and as classes change from year to year.

CONCLUSIONS

Our claim in 1971 that research into teaching methods in higher education would expand rapidly seems to have been justified. In the bibliography to the third edition of this monograph, 7 references had been published before 1950, 20 were from between 1950 and 1959, and over 280 from the decade from 1960 to 1969. In the fourth edition the number of references exceeds five hundred, despite omission of some earlier editions, and although the decade is not yet complete.

The growth of educational research has been accompanied in recent years by a growth in criticism of its methods and consequently of its results. There are so many variables that it is impossible to control all of them; even obviously important variables may sometimes remain uncontrolled. In addition, there are unpredictable effects. Human subjects when assigned to experimental and control groups differ from the biologists' wheat grains in being autonomous. They may choose to remove themselves, to compare notes with other students who are subjected to a different treatment; or they may so resent, or enjoy, a new method that their motivation and performance are significantly affected while it retains its novelty. Fatigue, pressure from other work, or some kind of distraction may also affect results. Even when experiments seem to be conducted successfully, the results usually apply only to certain groups of students. They provide little information about individuals and rarely establish causal relationships. And it is often difficult to draw conclusions having general application.

Sometimes the approach which comes nearest to obtaining generalisations is to compare results from many similar experiments. Thus, Hartley summarises findings from numerous experiments in programmed learning, and Bligh is able to judge the relative advantages of large and small classes by considering results of more than one hundred investigations. As we said in conclusion to the third edition, what is needed is a concerted effort in studying each teaching method, collating information already available and experimenting with variations of the method to see under what circumstances each is effective.

It seems unlikely that there will be a fifth edition of this monograph. As research results accumulate within the next few years, a series of volumes will be needed. Almost certainly there will be volumes on individualised learning and on evaluation of courses. Other volumes may be needed to survey results of experiments on study skills, the development of higher mental abilities, audio-visual aids and computers in teaching and learning, and, perhaps, of experiments in the use of simulation and games in teaching. There is already a volume on projects published by the Society for Research in Higher Education (Adderley et al, 1975).

Thus while it is true that we seem almost as far as ever from developing a theory of instruction, there is at least a fairly substantial body of information to provide ideas for teachers who wish to try new methods, and to indicate possible outcomes.

102

REFERENCES   'Pages' referred to are those in this volume

ABBOTT, F.R., COOK, G.B., HARTLEY, J.R., RAWSON, M., and SHAW,
M. (1972) 'Computer-based learning in the physical sciences'
Physics Education 7 (3) 136-142
Page 53

ABERCROMBIE, M.L.J. (1965) The anatomy of judgment London,
Hutchinson
Pages 64, 82

ABERCROMBIE, M.L.J. (1970) Aims and techniques of group teaching
London, Society for Research into Higher Education (3rd edition 1974)
Page 64

ADAMS, B.G., DANIEL, E.E., HERXHEIMER, A., and WEATHERALL, M.
(1960) 'The value of emphasis in eliminating errors' British
Medical Journal (2) 1007-1011
Pages 22, 38

ADDERLEY, K., ASHWIN, C., BRADBURY, P., FREEMAN, J.,
GOODLAD, S., GREENE, J., JENKINS, D., RAE, J., and UREN, O.
(1975) Project methods in higher education London, Society for
Research into Higher Education
Pages 7, 77, 100

ALDERMAN, G.H. (1926) 'Improving comprehension ability in silent reading'
Journal of Educational Research 13 (1) 11-21
Page 58

ALLEN, H.G. (1968) 'Engineering projects for engineering undergraduates'
in Innovations and experiments in university teaching methods
London, University Teaching Methods Research Unit
Page 75

ALLEN, P.S. (1975) 'A two channel slide method for lecture presentation'
Physics Education 10 (1) 52-55
Page 44

AMARIA, R.P., BIRAN, L.A., and LEITH, G.O.M. (1969) 'Individual
versus co-operative learning: I: influence of intelligence and sex'
Educational Research 11 (2) 95-103
Page 32

AMARIA, R.P., and LEITH, G.O.M. (1969) 'Individual versus co-operative
learning: II: the influence of personality' Educational Research
11 (3) 193-199
Page 32

AMSWYCH, R.J. (1967) 'The use of tape-recorded programmes for craft
training' Programmed Learning and Educational Technology 4 (4)
196-201
Page 35

ANDERSON, J. (1967) 'Testing clinical competence' British Journal of Medical Education 1 (5) 345-347
Page 85

ANDERSON, J., BUKITT, D., GEAL, M.A., and COCKER, P. (1968) 'How clinical students spend their time' British Journal of Medical Education 2 (1) 4-10
Page 21

ANDREW, R. (1975) 'An attempt at improvement in undergraduate teaching' International Journal of Electrical Engineering Education 12 (4) 298-301
Page 45

APPLEBY, E.C., and POLAND, J. (1968) 'Some observations on the use of tape-recorded programmes in teaching veterinary pathology' in UTMU (ed) Innovations and experiments in university teaching methods London, University Teaching Methods Research Unit
Page 45

APTER, M.J., and MURGATROYD, S. (1975) 'Concentration, personality, and self-pacing in programmed learning' Programmed Learning and Educational Technology 12 (4) 208-215
Page 31

ARMSTRONG, R.H.R., and TAYLOR, J. (eds) (1970) Instructional simulation systems in higher education (Cambridge Monographs on Teaching Methods, 2) Cambridge Institute of Education
Page 73

ASH, P., and CARLTON, B.J. (1953) 'The value of note-taking during film learning' British Journal of Educational Psychology 23 121-125
Page 51

ASHLEY, B. (1968) 'Group dynamics in human relations training' Case Conference 15 (2) 64-67
Page 82

AUSTRALIAN VICE-CHANCELLORS' COMMITTEE (1963) Teaching methods in Australian universities
Pages 40, 90, 92

BAILEY, A.G., BEYNON, J.D.E., and SIMS, G.D. (1975) 'Examinations and continuous assessment' International Journal of Electrical Engineering Education 12 (1) 13-24
Pages 25, 62

BARCLAY, T.B. (1957) 'Effective reading' University of Edinburgh Gazette 17 22-30
Page 57

BARNETT, S.A. (1958) 'An experiment with free-discussion groups' Universities Quarterly 12 (2) 175-180
Pages 68, 80

BARON, J. (1975) 'Some theories of college instruction' Higher Education
4 (2) 149-172
Page 94

BARRACLOUGH, B., and LIPSEET, V. (1972) 'Psychiatry for curates'
British Journal of Medical Education 6 (1) 20-21
Page 97

BARRINGTON, H. (1965) 'A survey of instructional television researches'
Educational Research 8 (1) 8-25
Page 49

BARRINGTON, H. (1971) 'An evaluation of the effectiveness of instructional
television presentation variables' British Journal of Educational
Psychology 41 (2) 219-220
Page 49

BATES, A. W. (1974) 'Success and failure in innovation at the Open
University' Programmed Learning and Educational Technology
11 (1) 16-23
Page 96

BAUME, A. D., and JONES, B. (1974) Education by objectives (Curricular
Study 1) London, Nelpress
Page 8

BEACH, L. R. (1974) 'Self-directed student groups and college learning'
Higher Education 3 (2) 187-200
Page 57

BEARD, R. M. (1967a) An inquiry into small group discussion methods in
three disciplines London, University Teaching Methods Research
Unit
Pages 11, 38, 63, 75

BEARD, R. M. (1967b) 'On evaluating the success of teaching' British
Journal of Medical Education 1 (4) 296-302
Pages 24, 66, 85, 89, 98

BEARD, R. M. (1969) 'A conspectus of research and development' in
Assessment of undergraduate performance London, Universities
Conference convened by the Committee of Vice-Chancellors and
Principals and the Association of University Teachers
Page 84

BEARD, R. M. (1976) Teaching and learning in higher education
Harmondsworth, Penguin

BEARD, R. M., HEALEY, F. G., and HOLLOWAY, P. J. (1974) Objectives
in higher education (3rd edition) London, Society for Research into
Higher Education
Page 10

BEARD, R. M., LEVY, P. M., and MADDOX, H. (1964) 'Academic performance at university' Educational Review 16 (3) 163-174 Pages 61, 88

BEARD, R. M., and POLE, K. (1971) 'The content and purpose of biochemistry examinations' British Journal of Medical Education (5) 13-21 Pages 13, 79, 84

BENNET, W. A. (1968) 'The use of closed-circuit television for second language teaching' in UTMU (ed) Innovations and experiments in university teaching methods London, University Teaching Methods Research Unit Page 51

BENT, H. A. (1974) 'No easy way: experience with a modified-Keller physical chemistry course' Journal of Chemical Education 51 (10) 661-664 Page 25

BERKOWITZ, L., LEVY, B. I., and HARVEY, A. R. (1957) 'Effects of performance evaluations on group integration and motivation' Human Relations 10 (2) 195-208 Page 65

BETHLEHEM, D. W. (1973) 'Prediction and improvement of academic performance in a developing country' British Journal of Educational Psychology 43 (3) 305-308 Page 56

BETTS, D. S., and WALTON, A. J. (1970) 'A lecture match or 'Anything you can do I can do better'' Physics Education 5 (6) 321-325 Page 40

BIRAN, L. A. (1966) 'A comparison of a scrambled and sequential presentation of a branching programme' Research Report on Programmed Learning 9 National Council for Programmed Learning, University of Birmingham Page 30

BIRAN, L. A., and PICKERING, E. (1968) 'Unscrambling a herringbone: an experimental evaluation of branching programming' British Journal of Medical Education (2) 213-9 Pages 17, 30

BLACK, J. (1974) Course scheme for BSc degrees in engineering, engineering with modern languages, and engineering with education University of Bath School of Engineering Page 13

BLACK, P. J. (1968) 'University examinations' Physics Education 3 (2) 93-99 Page 84

BLACK, P. J., DYSON, N. A., and O'CONNOR, D. A. (1968) 'Group studies'
Physics Education 3 (6) 289-293
Page 76

BLACK, P. J., GRIFFITH, J. A. R., and POWELL, W. B. (1974) 'Skills
sessions' Physics Education 9 (1) 18-22
Page 56

BLAUG, M. (1968) Universities and productivity Universities Conference,
March 1968. Convened by the Committee of Vice-Chancellors and
Principals and the Association of University Teachers (London)
Page 14

BLIGH, D. A. (1970a) 'The case for a variety of teaching methods in each
lesson' British Journal of Medical Education 4 (3) 202-209
Page 40

BLIGH, D. A. (1970b) 'A pilot experiment to test the relative effectiveness
of three kinds of teaching methods' Research in Librarianship
3 (15) 88-93
Page 45

BLIGH, D. A. (1971) 'Teaching students in groups' (Typescript available
from University Teaching Methods Unit, University of London Institute
of Education)
Page 89

BLIGH, D. A. (1972a) What's the use of lectures? Harmondsworth, Penguin
Pages 15, 37

BLIGH, D. A. (1972b) 'Teaching decisions with small groups in large classes'
London Educational Review 1 (1) 69-74
Page 73

BLIGH, D. A. (1973) 'Techniques in small group discussion' in BLIGH, D. A.
(ed) Background papers: introductory course for lecturers London,
University Teaching Methods Unit
Page 63

BLIGH, D. A. (1974) 'Are varied teaching methods more effective?'
(PhD thesis) University of London
Pages 15, 37, 38, 39, 40, 43, 45, 48, 50, 89

BLIGH, D. A. (1975a) Gropings for a design of objective tests of the effectiveness of teaching methods London, University Teaching Methods Unit
Page 89

BLIGH, D. A. (1975b) 'The reliability yet invalidity of students' opinions of
teaching' (Paper read to the British Psychological Society Education
Section at Sheffield) Exeter University Teaching Services
Pages 36, 37, 43

BLIGH, D.A., EBRAHIM, J.G., JAQUES, D., and WARREN PIPER, D.
(1975) Teaching students Exeter University Teaching Services
Pages 8, 21, 32, 63, 66

BLIZARD, P.J., and BLUNT, M.J. (1975) The development, initial and
long-term assessment of a teaching-learning programme in anatomy
University of New South Wales Tertiary Educational Research Centre
Page 8

BLOOM, B.S. (ed) (1956) Taxonomy of educational objectives: I: cognitive
domain New York, David McKay
Pages 8, 29

BLUNT, J.M., and BLIZARD, P.J. (1973) 'Development and initial assessment of a teaching-learning programme in anatomy' British Journal
of Medical Education 7 (4) 244-250
Pages 24, 96

BOUD, D.J. (1973) 'The laboratory aims questionnaire — new method for
course improvement' Higher Education 2 (1) 81-94
Page 11

BOUD, D.J. (1976) Objectives in applied science education (Report to the
Leverhulme Trust)
Page 13

BRANDT, D., ANSELL, M., and CRYER, N.B. (1974) 'Minicourses in a
first year physics lab.' Physics Education 9 (1) 23-26
Page 45

BREWER, I.M. (1974) 'Recall, comprehension and problem solving:
evaluation of an audio-visual method of learning plant anatomy'
Journal of Biological Education 8 (2) 101-112
Pages 24, 96

BRISTOW, T (1970) 'A reading seminar' The Library College Journal
3 (3) 13-22

BRITISH MEDICAL STUDENTS'ASSOCIATION (1965) Report on medical
education: suggestions for the future London, British Medical
Association
Pages 27, 35, 91

BROCKBANK, J.P. (1969) 'New assessment techniques in use — the arts'
in Assessment of undergraduate performance Universities Conference
convened by the Committee of Vice-Chancellors and Principals of the
Association of University Teachers, London
Page 85

BROWN, G.A. (1976a) Microteaching. Impetus. Newsletter No.4 2-11
Page 50

BROWN, G. A. (1976b) 'Using microteaching to train new lecturers'
University Vision (15) 24-31

BRYANT, K. H. J., and HOARE, D. E. (1970) First year chemistry in
Australian universities The Australian Vice-Chancellors'
Committee
Page 79

BUCKLEY-SHARP, M. D., HARRIS, F. T. C., TEPSON, J. B., SMITH,
W. R. D., and WALKER, S. (1969) 'The evaluation of a programmed
learning course' British Journal of Medical Education 3 (2) 151-154
Page 30

BURKE, R. J. (1969) 'Some preliminary data on the use of self-evaluations
and peer ratings in assigning university course grades' Journal of
Educational Research 62 (10) 444-448
Page 66

BURKE, W. H. (1967) 'The new course and its development' Design
Education (2) 19-24
Page 10

CANTRELL, E. G. (1971) 'Thirty lectures' British Journal of Medical
Education 5 (4) 300-319
Page 89

CARPENTER, N. (1975) 'Continuous assessment and student motivation
in management studies' International Journal of Electrical
Engineering Education 12 (1) 5-12
Pages 25, 62

CARRE, C. G. (1969) 'Audio-tutorials as adjuncts to formal lecturing in
biology teaching at the tertiary level' Journal of Biological
Education 3 (1) 57-64
Page 46

CARTER, G., and LEE, L. S. (1975) 'A study of attitudes to first year
undergraduate electrical engineering laboratory work at the
University of Salford International Journal of Electrical Engineering
Education 12 (3) 278-289
Page 56

CASTLE, W., and DAVIDSON, L. (1969) 'An evaluation of programmed
instruction in a new medical faculty' British Journal of Medical
Education 3 (4) 359-361
Page 31

de CECCO, P. (1964) 'Class size and co-ordinated instruction' British
Journal of Educational Psychology 34 (1) 65-74
Page 14

CENTRE FOR INFORMATION OF LANGUAGE TEACHING (1974) Survey
of research and materials development in vocational uses of English,
French and German   See LUNT, H. (ed)
Pages 46-47

CHADWICK, G. (1974) 'Students may decide course objectives themselves'
Times Higher Education Supplement   3 May 1974
Page 7

CHALMERS, R.A., and STARK, J. (1968) 'Continuous assessment of
practical work in the Scottish HNC course in chemistry'   Education
in Chemistry 5 (4) 154-155
Page 78

CHILD, D. (1970) 'Some aspects of study habits on higher education'
International Journal of Educational Science 4 (1) 11-20
Page 20

CHU, G.H., and SCHRAMM, W. (1967) 'Learning from television: what the
research says' Stanford Institute for Communication Research
Pages 14, 48

CLOSSICK, M. (1967) 'Student residence: a new approach at the University
of Essex' London, Society for Research into Higher Education
Page 21

COEKIN, J.A. (1970) 'Teamwork with an industrial context in the second
year electronics laboratory' International Journal of Engineering
Education 8 (2) 123-125
Page 75

COLES, P., and FOSTER, J. (1975) 'Typographic cueing as an aid to
learning from typewritten text' Programmed Learning and
Educational Technology 12 (2) 102-108
Page 60

COLLARD, M., GRIFFITH, J., LIDDY, H., SHUK, V., and SWINBURNE, E.S.
(1969) 'The use of models and programmed learning in organic
chemistry' Education in Chemistry 6 (4) 130-132
Page 18

COLLIER, K.G. (1966) 'An experiment in university teaching' Universities
Quarterly 20 (3) 336-348
Page 76

COLLIER, K.G. (1969) 'Syndicate methods: further evidence and comments'
Universities Quarterly 23 (4) 431-436
Page 76

COMMITTEE ON HIGHER EDUCATION (1963) Higher education   London,
HMSO
Page 6

110

CONNOR, D.J. (1968) 'Teaching engineering students by machine and text' Programmed Learning and Educational Technology 5 (2) 129-135
Page 34

CONNOR, D.V. (1967) 'A study of problem solving in physics' Australian Journal of Higher Education 3 (1) 55-67
Page 74

CONNORS, B. (1972) 'Testing innovations in course design' British Journal of Educational Technology 1 (3) 48-52
Page 67

COOMBS, M.J. (1974) 'The promotion of learning from complex televisual materials by the use of expectancies' Programmed Learning and Educational Technology 11 (3) 133-139
Page 26

COOPER, C.L. (1968) 'A study of the role of the staff trainer in human relations training groups' (Unpublished PhD thesis) University of Leeds, Department of Management
Page 81

COOPER, B., and FOY, J.M. (1967) 'Evaluating the effectiveness of lectures' Universities Quarterly 21 (2) 182-185
Page 42

COOPER, B., and FOY, J.M. (1969) 'Students' study habits, attitudes and academic attainment' Universities Quarterly 23 (2) 203-212
Page 21

COPE, E. (1969) 'Students and school practice' Education for Teaching No. 88 23-25 Autumn 1969
Page 12

COPELAND, W.D. (1975) 'The relationship between microteaching and student-teacher classroom performance' Journal of Educational Research 68 (8) 289-293
Page 50

CORNWALL, M.G. (1975) 'Authority versus experience in higher education: project orientation in some Continental universities' Universities Quarterly 29 (3) 372-398
Pages 13, 76

COSTIN, F. (1972) 'Lecturing versus other methods in teaching' British Journal of Educational Technology 1 (3) 4-31
Page 38

COTTRELL, T.L. (1962) 'Effect of size of tutorial group on teaching efficiency' University of Edinburgh Gazette 33 20-21
Page 15

COWAN, J., McCONNELL, S. G., and BOLTON, A. (1970) 'Learner directed group work for large classes' Heriot-Watt University Department of Civil Engineering Pages 51, 76, 79

COWAN, J., and MORTON, J. (1973) 'MOCO — a structural game for undergraduates' Programmed Learning and Educational Technology 10 (4) 267-273 Page 72

COWIE, A. P., and HEATON, J. B. (eds) (1977) English for academic purposes: papers on the language problems of overseas students in higher education in the UK BAAL (British Association for Applied Linguistics) SELMOUS Page 47

COX, M., ELTON, L. R. D., and GRAY, R. G. (1974) 'Use of computer methods in an introductory quantum mechanics course' International Journal of Mathematical Education 5 (2) 157-160 Page 19

COX, R. (1967) 'Examinations and higher education' Universities Quarterly 21 (3) 292-340 Page 84

COX, R. J., and KONTIAINEN, S. (1974) 'Comparison of attitudes of trained trainers, untrained trainers, and trainees in general practice' British Journal of Medical Education 8 (2) 103-111 Page 97

COYLE, J. D., and SERVANT, D. M. (1975) 'A film-based notional practical' Education in Chemistry 12 (3) 82-83 Page 54

CRAIG, W. R. (1968) 'Experiment in television teaching and its reaction' International Journal of Electrical Engineering Education 6 (2) 306-8 Page 48

CROMBAG, H. F. M., DE WIJKERSLOOTH, J. L., and VAN TUYLL VAN SEROOSKERKEN (1972) 'On solving legal problems' in Over het oplosson van casusposities Gronignen, H. D. Tjeenk Willink Page 72

CROSSLAND, A. (1967) Speech by the Secretary of State for Education and Science, University of Lancaster Page 6

CROSSLEY, C. A. (1968) 'Tuition in the use of the library and of subject literature in the University of Bradford' Journal of Documentation 24 (2) 91-97 Page 61

CROWN, S., LUCAS, C. J., and SUPRAMANIAM, S. (1973) 'The delineation and measurement of study difficulty in university students' British Journal of Psychiatry 122 (569) 381-393 and British Journal of Guidance and Counselling Abstracts 2 (2) No. 237
Page 57

CROXTON, P. C. L., and MARTIN, L. H. (1965) 'Away with notes' : (Programming in Higher Education) New Education (I) 25-27
Page 34

CROXTON, P. C. L., and MARTIN, L. H. (1968) 'Progressive evaluation and the control of programmed classes in degree courses' in TOBIN, M. J. (ed) Problems and methods in programmed learning Proceedings of the Association of Programmed Learning/National Centre for Programmed Learning 1967 Birmingham Conference (3) 83
Page 34

CRUIKSHANK, D. R. (1963) 'Simulation' Theory into Practice 7 (5) 190-193
Page 73

CULLEN, J. B. (1973) 'Social identity and motivation' Psychological Reports 33 (1) 338
Page 83

CURETON, L. (1968) 'T-groups, inter-groups in teacher training' (Unpublished MPhil thesis) University of Sussex
Page 80

DALLOS, R. (1975) 'Programmed learning and personality: a review and a preliminary study' Programmed Learning and Educational Technology 12 (1) 12-20
Page 31

DAVEY, A. G. (1969) 'Leadership in relation to group achievement' Educational Research 11 (3) 185-192
Page 65

DAVIDSON, J. K., and THOMPSON, G. D. B. (1970) 'Closed-circuit tele- vision in teaching diagnostic radiology' British Journal of Medical Education 4 (1) 23-28
Page 94

DAVIE, R. S., and RUSSELL, J. K. (1974) 'Attitudes and abilities of co-operative students' The Australian Journal of Education 18 (2) 150-171
Page 95

DAVIES, B. M., and MOWBRAY, R. M. (1968) 'Medical students' personality and academic achievement' British Journal of Medical Education 2 (3) 195-199
Page 86

DAVIES, G. N. (1967) 'Changing concepts in dental education' New Zealand Dental Journal (63) 107-112
Page 80

DEAN, T. M. (1971) 'Medical students' responses to undergraduate instruction in general practice' British Journal of Medical Education 5 (4) 269-272
Page 99

DEUTSCH, M. (1949) 'Experimental study of effects of co-operation and competition upon group process Human Relations 2 (3) 199-231
Page 65

DICK, W. (1963) 'Retention as a function of paired and individual use of programmed instruction' Journal of Programmed Instruction 2 (3) 17-23
Pages 32, 33

DIGGINS, F. W. E. (1974) 'The use of haemoglobin as a model for teaching the relationship between structure and function' Journal of Biological Education 8 (5) 250-8
Page 28

de DOMBAL, F. T., HARTLEY, J. R., and SLEEMAN, D. H. (1969) 'A computer-assisted system for learning clinical diagnosis' The Lancet 1969 1 Jan 18 145-148
Page 53

DONALDSON, G. W. (1974) Teaching and assessing 200 2nd-year electrical engineering students International Journal of Electrical Engineering Education Vol. 11 (3) 223-226
Page 25

DOSKIN, V. A., and LAURENT'EVA, N. A. (First Moscow Institute) (1974) 'Rizm fiziologicheskikh funktsu i rezhim obucheniya' (The rhythm of physiological functions and teaching arrangements) Vestnik vysshei shkoly (5) 76-79
Page 15

DOWDESWELL, W. H. (1970) 'Inter-university biology teaching project' Journal of Biological Education 4 (3) 197-203
Page 78

DOWDESWELL, W. H. (1972) 'Inter-university biology project' Nature 238 (5363) 313-315
Page 9

DUBIN, R., and HEDLEY, R. A. (1969) 'The medium may be relegated to the message: college instruction by T. V.' Eugene, University of Oregon Press
Page 48

DUDLEY, H. A. F. (1970) 'Taxonomy of clinical educational objectives' British Journal of Medical Education 4 (1) 13-18
Page 12

DUNN, W. R. (1969) 'Programmed learning news: feedback devices in university lectures' New University 3 (4) 21-22
Page 24

ECKERT, R. E., and NEALE, D. C. (1965) 'Teachers and teaching' Review of Educational Research 35 304-317
Page 3

EDWARDS, C. H. (1967) 'Experience with an integrated first six months clinical training' in UTMU (ed) Teaching for efficient learning (report of a conference held at the University of London Institute of Education) London, University Teaching Methods Research Unit
Page 76

EDWARDS, C. H. (1975) 'Changing teacher behaviour through self-instruction and supervised micro-teaching in a competency based programme' Journal of Educational Research 68 (6) 219-222
Page 50

EGGLESTON, J. E. (1969) 'A strategy for the identification and communication of teaching objectives in sociology' in UTMU (ed) Conference on objectives in higher education London, University Teaching Methods Research Unit
Page 12

EGGLESTON, J. F., and KELLEY, P. J. (1970) 'The assessment of project work in A-level biology' Educational Research 12 (3) 225-229
Page 77

ELKINS, T. H. (1974) 'Developments in interdisciplinarity' Group for Research and Innovation in Higher Education Newsletter No. 4 London, The Nuffield Foundation
Page 7

ELLEY, W. B. (1966) 'The role of errors in learning with feedback' British Journal of Educational Psychology 31 (3) 296-300
Page 23

ELLIOTT, A. G. P. (1958) An experiment in group dynamics (mimeograph) Simon Eng., Ltd.
Page 81

ELLIS, H. P., and JONES, A. D. (1974) 'Anxiety about lecturing' Universities Quarterly 29 (1) 91-95
Page 35

ELTON, C. F. (1965) 'The effect of logic instruction on the Valentine Reasoning Test' British Journal of Educational Psychology 35 (3) 339-341
Page 69

ELTON, L. R. B. (1968) 'The assessment of students — a new approach' Universities Quarterly 23 (3) 291-301
Page 85

ELTON, L. R. B., HILLS, P. J., and O'CONNELL, S. (1970) 'Self-teaching situations in a university physics course' in International congress on the education of teachers of physics in secondary schools Eger, Hungary
Pages 25, 76, 92

ENGEL, C. E., LOWE, G. D. O., MARSHALL, P. B., and WAKEFORD, R. E. (1974) 'Teaching basic pharmacology to medical students: an experimental self-instructional approach' in Medical and Biological Illustration 24 (3) 130-134
Page 45

ENTWISTLE, N. J., and ENTWISTLE, D. (1970) 'The relationship between personality, study methods, and academic performance' British Journal of Educational Psychology 40 (2) 132-143
Page 86

ENTWISTLE, N. J., PERCY, K. A., and NISBET, J. B. (1971) Educational objectives and academic performance in higher education (summary of a preliminary report) University of Lancaster Department of Educational Research
Pages 6, 11, 20, 21

EPSTEIN, H. T. (1970) A strategy for education Oxford University Press
Page 28

EPSTEIN, H. T. (1972) 'An experiment in education' Nature 235 Jan 28 203-205
Page 28

ERAUT, M. (1970) 'Course development: an approach to the improvement of teaching in higher education' Journal of Educational Technology 1 (3) 195-206
Page 8

ERSKINE, C. A., and O'MORCHOE, C. C. C. (1961) 'Research on teaching methods: its significance for the curriculum' The Lancet 1961 2 Sept 23 709-711
Page 22

ERSKINE, C. A., and TOMKIN, A. (1963) 'Evaluation of the effect of the group discussion method in a complex teaching programme' Journal of Medical Education (38) 1036-1042
Page 17

FALK, B. (1967) 'The use of student evaluation' The Australian University 5 (2) 109-121
Page 99

FARRELL, W. H. (1965) 'Programmed learning in the Royal Canadian Air Force' Programmed Learning 2 (3) 176-181
Page 29

FELDMAN, K. A., and NEWCOMB, T. M. (1973) The impact of college on students: Volume 1 Jossey Bass
Page 94

FLEMING, J. (1975) 'Computer-aided design teaching experiment' (Strathclyde Department of Architecture)

FLETCHER, S., and WATSON, A. A. (1968) 'Magnetic tape recording in the teaching of histopathology British Journal of Medical Education 2 (4) 283-292
Page 45

FLOOD PAGE, C. (1971) Technical Aids to Teaching in Higher Education London, Society for Research into Higher Education (2nd edition 1976)
Pages 43, 52, 53

FLOOD PAGE, C. (1974) Student evaluation of teaching: the American experience London, Society for Research into Higher Education
Page 42

FORSYTH, H. A. (1973) 'Computers as an aid to teaching nutrition' Journal of Biological Education 7 (3) 31-36
Page 53

FOSTER, J. (1968) 'A note on the visibility of black-on-white and white-on-black photographic slides' British Psychological Society Bulletin 21 (72) 173
Page 43

FOULDS, K. W. H., HARLOW, R. G., JACKSON, D. F., and WHORLOW, R. W (1969) 'Undergraduate physics projects at the University of Surrey' Physics Education 4 (6) 344-345
Page 76

FOY, J. M. (1969) 'A note on lecturer evaluation by students' Universities Quarterly 23 (3) 345-348
Pages 42, 88

FRANCIS, R. D., COLLINS, J., and CASSEL, A. J. (1973) 'The effect of reading tuition on academic achievement: volunteering and methods of tuition' British Journal of Educational Psychology 43 (3) 298-300
Pages 57, 58

FREEMAN, J., and BYRNE, P. S. (1973) The assessment of post-graduate training in general practice London, Society for Research into Higher Education
Pages 12, 97

FREYBERG, P. S. (1956) 'The effectiveness of note-taking' Education for Teaching 39 February 17-24
Page 59

FRY, E. (1963a) Teaching faster reading London, Cambridge University Press
Page 57

FRY, E. (1963b) Reading faster London, Cambridge University Press
Page 57

GAGNE, R. (1965) The conditions of learning Holt, Rinehart & Winston
Page 28

GALLEGOS, A. M. (1968) 'Experimenter pacing and student pacing of programmed instruction' Journal of Educational Research 61 (8) 339-342
Page 33

GANE, C. P. (1969) 'Educational technology v. the technology of education' The Royal Television Society Journal 12 (5) 101-104
Page 26

GANE, C. P., HORABIN, I. S., and LEWIS, B. N. (1966) 'The simplification and avoidance of instruction' Industrial Training International July
Page 70

GARBUTT, D. (1963) 'An investigation into students' understanding of some accountancy terms' The Vocational Aspect of Secondary and Further Education 31 (15) 69-169
Pages 55, 69

GARDINER, Q., BODDY, F. A., and TAYLOR, J. (1969) 'An orientation course for first-year medical students' British Journal of Medical Education 3 (3) 199-202
Page 20

GAUVAIN, S. (1968) 'The use of student opinion in the quality control of teaching' British Journal of Medical Education 2 (1) 55-62
Page 98

GAUVAIN, S. (1970) Questionnaire techniques in course evaluation (paper given to Symposium on Automation in Medical and other Higher Education, Multiple-Choice Questions and Research, June 1970)
Page 98

GAUVAIN, S., WOOD, C.H., WALFORD, J., and SCHILLING, R.S.F. (1965) 'Experiment in postgraduate education to evaluate teaching and examining techniques' Journal of Medical Education 40 (1) 516-523
Page 98

GESSNER, F.B. (1974) 'An experiment in modified self-paced learning' English Education 64 (5) 368-370
Page 97

GIBB, G.O. (1968) 'Account of an experiment designed to test the effectiveness of a commentary superimposed over a televised classroom situation' Educational Television International 2 (2) 173-179
Page 49

GIBSON, J.N. (1970) 'Paper in a symposium on attitude measurement in exploratory studies' Bulletin of the British Psychological Society 23 (81) 323-324
Page 69

GILBERT, T. (1975) 'The effect of dictated notes on the recall and comprehension of connected and disconnected verbal material' British Journal of Educational Technology 1 (6) 62-65
Page 59

GILLILAND, I.C., and GIBBONS, J.L. (1971) 'The assessment of advanced courses of medical education' British Journal of Medical Education 5 (4) 305-306
Page 97

GLYNN, E. (1965) 'Keys to chemistry (a personal effort in programming)' New Education (I) 21-22
Page 32

GOMES da COSTA, B., SMITH, T.M.F., and WHITELEY, D. (1974) 'German language attainment: a sample survey of universities and colleges in the UK' N.E. London Polytechnic
Page 47

GOODHUE, D. (1969) 'Tape-recorded lectures with slide synchronization: a description of the method' Journal of Biological Education 3 (4) 311-319
Page 54

GOODLAD, S. (1970) 'Project work in developing countries: a British experiment in engineering education' International Journal of Electrical Engineering Education 8 (2) 135-140
Page 75

GORBUTT, D. (1974) 'The new sociology of education' in REID, I., and WORMALD, E. (eds) Sociology and teacher education Social Science Section: Association of Teachers in Colleges and Departments of Education (London)
Page 1

GRADDON, J., SNOW, T., and WATTS, A.G. (1974) 'Careers education in higher education: an experiment'. British Journal of Guidance and Counselling 2 (1) 96-100
Page 73

GRAVES, J. and V. (eds) (1963) Report on conference on the use of tape in medical teaching at the College of General Practitioners Chelmsford, Royal College of General Practitioners Medical Recording Service and Sound Library
Page 44

GRAVES, J. and V. (1965) Medical sound recording London and New York, Focal Press
Page 44

GRAVES, J. and V. (eds) (1967) Report on second conference on the use of audiotape in medical teaching Chelmsford, Royal College of General Practitioners Medical Recording Service and Sound Library
Page 44

GRUBB, R.E. (1968) 'Learner-controlled statistics' Programmed Learning and Educational Technology 5 (1) 38-42
Page 53

GRUGEON, D. et al (1972) Draft unit on course tuition Open University
Page 25

GRUNEBERG, M.M., and STARTUP, R. (1975) 'First year university students' preconceptions of their teacher's week' Vocational Aspect of Education XXVII (67) 45-48
Page 88

GUILD, R.E. (1966) 'An experiment in modified programmed self-instruction' Journal of Dental Education 30 (2) 181-189
Page 30

GUST, T., and SCHUMACHER, D. (1969) 'Handwriting speed of college students' Journal of Educational Research 62 (5) 198-200
Page 40

HALE, P.R. (1965) 'Using closed-circuit television' Cambridge Institute of Education Bulletin 3 (1) 5-11
Page 50

HALL, W.C. (1975) 'De-mystifying curriculum development' Universities Quarterly 29 (2) 166-170
Page 9

HALSEY, A.H., and TROW, M. (1971) The British academics London, Faber
Page 88

HALLWORTH, H.J. (1957) 'Group discussion in its relevance to teacher training' Educational Review 10 (1) 41-53
Page 80

HAMMERSLEY, J. H. (1968) 'On the enfeeblement of mathematical skills by 'modern mathematics' and by similar soft track in schools and universities' Bulletin of the Institute of Mathematics and its Application 4 (4) 1-22
Page 78

HANDY, J., and JOHNSTONE, A. (1974) 'Project assessment' Education in Chemistry 11 (2) 56-57
Page 77

HANSON, R.W., and SIMMONS, G.A.E. (1972) 'An integrated laboratory project' Chemistry in Britain 9 (2) 58-59
Page 77

HARDEN, R. McG., DUNN, W. R., HOLROYD, C., LEVER, R., LINDSAY, A., and WILSON, G. M. (1969) 'An experiment involving substitution of tape/slide programmes for lectures' The Lancet 1969 1 May 3 933-935
Page 18

HARDEN, R. McG., WAYNE, Sir E., and DONALD, G. (1968) 'An audio-visual technique for medical teaching' Journal of Medical and Biological Illustration 18 (1) 29-32
Page 46

HARDING, A. G. (1973a) 'The objectives and structure of undergraduate projects' British Journal of Educational Technology 4 (2) 94-105
Pages 13, 77

HARDING, A. G. (1973b) 'The project: its place as a learning situation' British Journal of Educational Technology 4 (3) 216-232
Page 77

HARDING, A. G., and SAYER, S. (1975) 'The objectives of training university teachers' Universities Quarterly 3 Summer 299-317
Page 13

HARGREAVES, S. (1970) 'The Esso students' business game' The Technical Journal 8 (5) 14-16
Page 73

HARRISON, M. I. (1968) 'A computer-based learning system' Design Electronics 5 (1) 30-33
Page 53

HARTLEY, J. R. (1968) 'An experiment showing some student benefits against behavioural costs in using programmed learning' Programmed Learning and Educational Technology 5 (3) 219
Page 16

HARTLEY, J. (1968) 'Some factors affecting student performance in programmed learning' Programmed Learning and Educational Technology 5 (3) 206-218
Pages 32, 33

HARTLEY, J. (1974a) 'Programmed instruction 1954-74: a review' Programmed Learning and Educational Technology 11 (6) 273-291
Page 32

HARTLEY, J. (1974b) 'Psychology teaching' Bulletin for the Association for the Teaching of Psychology 2 (1) 206-250
Page 96

HARTLEY, J. (1976) 'Lecture handouts and student note-taking' Programmed Learning and Educational Technology (in press)
Page 59

HARTLEY, J., and CAMERON, A. (1967) 'Some observations on the efficiency of lecturing' Educational Review 20 (1) 30-37
Page 59

HARTLEY, J., and MARSHALL, S. (1974) 'On notes and note-taking' Universities Quarterly 28 (2) 225-235
Page 60

HAWKINS, J.D. (1969) 'A survey of student opinion on practical biochemistry' in WILLS, E.D. (ed) Practical biochemistry in the medical course (report of the Federation of European Biochemical Societies at St. Bartholomew's Hospital, London)
Page 91

HAWKRIDGE, D. (1974) 'Problems in implementing computer managed learning' British Journal of Educational Technology 5 (1) 31-43
Page 53

HAYES, D.M. (1964) 'Objective evaluation of a subjective teaching method: the student dissertation' Journal of Medical Education (39) 1083-1089
Pages 76, 77

HAYTHORN, W., COUCH, A., HAEFNER, D., LANGHAM, P., and LANNOR, F.C. (1956) 'The behaviour of authoritarian and egalitarian personalities in groups' Human Relations 9 (1) 57-74
Page 65

HEARNSHAW, T., and ROACH, D.K. (1974) 'A self instructional course in audio-visual techniques' British Journal of Educational Technology 3 (5) 60-72
Page 96

HELFER, R.E., and SLATER, C.H. (1971) 'Measuring the process of solving clinical diagnostic problems' British Journal of Medical Education 5 (1) 48-52
Page 72

HENSHAW, E. M., LANGDON, J., and HOLMAN, P. (1933) Manual dexterity: effects of training (Independent Health Research Board Report 67) London, HMSO
Page 55

HEWARD, C., MASH, V., and HEYWOOD, J. (1968) 'Student reaction to sandwich courses for the diploma in technology' Bulletin of Mechanical Engineering Education 7 (3) 253-268
Page 20

HEYWOOD, J., YOUNGMAN, M. B., MONK, J. D., and OXTOBY, R. (1973) Summary and results of an investigation into the classification of objectives for the training of technologists and technicians (Industrial Research Training Project) University of Lancaster Department of Educational Research
Page 13

HEYWOOD, J. (1975) 'Towards the classification of objectives in training technologists and technicians' International Journal of Electrical Engineering Education 12 (3) 217-233
Page 13

HILL, K. R., and SCHEUER, P. J. (1965) 'A rapid reading course' Royal Free Hospital Journal (29) 23-25
Page 57

HIRST, K., and BIGGS, N. (1969) 'Undergraduate projects in mathematics' Educational Studies in Mathematics 1 (3) 252-261
Pages 76, 77

HOARE, D. E., and INGLIS, G. R. (1965) 'Programmed learning in chemistry: II: an experiment' Education in Chemistry 2 (1) 32-35
Page 29

HOARE, D. E., and REVANS, M. M. (1969) 'Measuring attainment of educational objectives in chemistry' Education in Chemistry 6 (3) 78-80
Page 29

HOBEROEK, J. L. (1971) 'Personalised instruction in mechanical engineering' Journal of Engineering Education 81 (6) 506-507
Page 97

HOGG, D. R. (1973) 'Student attitudes to programmed learning' Education in Chemistry 10 (1) 7-9
Page 30

HOLGATE, A. (1971) 'Teaching design to engineers: presentation and reception' Australian Journal of Higher Education 4 (2) 110-115
Page 99

HOLLAND, W. W., GARRAD, J., BENNETT, A. E., and RHODES, P. (1966) 'A clinical approach to the teaching of social medicine: an evaluation of an experimental method' The Lancet 1966 1 Mar 5 540-542
Page 27

HOLLOWAY, P. J. (1964) 'A test of the use of a teaching aid for the instruction of undergraduate dental students in operative techniques' The Dental Practitioner 14 375-377
Page 44

HOLLOWAY, P. J. (1966) 'The effect of lecture time on learning' British Journal of Educational Psychology 31 (3) 255-258
Page 38

HOLMES, E. L. (1970) 'Co-operative engineering education at the University of Waterloo' International Journal of Electrical Engineering Education 8 (1) 3-10
Page 20

HOLMES, P. G. (1969) 'An open-ended electrical machine laboratory for second-year undergraduates' International Journal of Electrical Engineering 7 (3/4) 431-437
Page 75

HOOPER, R. (1974) 'The computer's role as a manager of learning' Education 144 (16) 454-456
Page 19

HOOS, I. R. (1975) 'The costs of efficiency: implications of educational technology' Journal of Higher Education 46 (2) 141-159
Page 14

HOPKINS, A. D. (1967) The training of professional metallurgists (Lancaster Studies in Higher Education No. 2) University of Lancaster
Page 13

HORNSBY-SMITH, M. P. (1973) 'Styles of teaching and their influence upon the interests of students in science' Durham Research Review 7 (31) 807-815
Page 37

HOUSTON, J. G., and PILLINER, A. E. (1974) 'The effect of verbal teaching style on the attainment of educational objectives in physics' British Journal of Educational Psychology 44 (2) 163-173
Page 37

HOWE, M. J. A. (1974) 'The utility of taking notes as an aid to learning' Educational Research 16 (3) 222-227
Page 60

HOWE, J. and SINGER, L. (1975) 'Presentation variables and student's activities in meaningful learning' British Journal of Educational Psychology 45 (1) 52-61
Page 58

HUBER, Paul B. (1974) 'An internal measure of productivity in the university' Dalhousie University Department of Economics
Page 21

HUDSON, L. (1966) Contrary imaginations: a psychological study of the English schoolboy London, Methuen
Pages 74, 75

HUGHES, D. O., and MORGAN, E. D. (1970) 'A student exercise in X-ray crystallography' Education in Chemistry 7 (2) 59-61
Page 78

INHELDER, B., and PIAGET, J. (1958) The growth of logical thinking London, Routledge and Kegan Paul
Page 69

IVEY, A. E. (1974) 'Microcounselling: teacher training as facilitation of pupil growth' British Journal of Educational Technology 2 (5) 16-21
Page 50

JAHODA, M., and THOMAS, L. F. (1966) 'The mechanics of learning' New Scientist 30 April 14 114-117
Page 58

JAMES, D. W., JOHNSON, M. L. (now ABERCROMBIE, M. L. J.), and VENNING, P. (1956) 'Testing for learnt skill in observation and evaluation of evidence' The Lancet 1956 2 Aug 25 379-383
Page 68

JAMES, P. E. (1970) 'A comparison of the efficiency of programmed video-tape and instruction booklet in learning to operate a desk calculator' Programmed Learning and Educational Technology 7 (2) 134-139
Pages 32, 33, 35, 94

JAMIESON, D. W., and THOMAS, K. W. (1974) 'Power and conflict in the student/teacher relationship' Sociology of Education Abstracts 10 (4) 707
Page 98

JAMIESON, G. H., JAMES, P. E., and LEYTHAM, G. W. H. (1969) 'Comparisons between teaching methods at the postgraduate level' Programmed Learning 6 (4) 243-244
Page 30

JEFFRIES, T. O., and LEECH, D. J. (1969) 'A student design contract' International Journal of Electrical Engineering Education 7 (2) 182-191
Page 75

JENKINS, D. E. P. (1968) 'The efficient use of laboratory time in the teaching of engineering' in Innovations and Experiments in University Teaching Methods London, University Teaching Methods Research Un
Page 79

JEPSON, J. (1969) 'Some methods of teaching practical biochemistry' in WILLS, E. D. (ed) Practical biochemistry in the medical course Report of the Federal European Biochemical Society Summer School, April 1968
Page 79

JEWELL, B. R. (1970) 'Logistics of organizing a practical course' British Journal of Medical Education 4 (3) 210-215
Page 79

JOHNSON, H. C., RHODES, D. H., and RUMERY, R. H. (1975) 'The assessment of teaching in higher education' Higher Education 4 (2) 173-200
Page 89

JOHNSTON, J. O., and CALHOUN, J. A. P. (1969) 'The serial position effect in lecture material' Journal of Educational Research 62 (6) 255-258
Page 39

JOHNSTONE, R. E. (1974) 'A note on students' design projects' Chemical Engineer (286) 390

JONES, G. (1965) 'Organic research projects in an undergraduate course' Education in Chemistry 2 (5) 238-240
Page 75

JONES, G. O. (1969) 'Physics in the new London BSc degree' Physics Education 4 (3) 143-150
Page 13

JONES, L., and WYLIE, A. (1976) 'Routes for part time study: student wastage and comparative costs' Education and Training 18 (3) 77-79, 82
Page 20

JOYCE, C. R. B., and WEATHERALL, M. (1957) 'Controlled experiments in teaching The Lancet 1957 2 402-407
Pages 17, 94

JOYCE, C. R. B., and WEATHERALL, M. (1959) 'Effective use of teaching time' The Lancet 1959 1 Mar 14 568-571
Pages 17, 36, 93

JOYCE, C. R. B., and HUDSON, L. (1968) 'Student style and teacher style' British Journal of Medical Education 2 (1) 28-31
Pages 74, 83

KALLENBACH, W. W., and GALL, M. D. (1969) 'Microteaching vs conventional methods in training elementary intern teachers' Journal of Educational Research 63 (3) 136-141
Page 50

KANDEL, I. (1936) Examinations and their substitutes in the United States New York, Carnegie Foundation for the Advancement of Teaching (Bulletin 28)
Page 62

KATZ, F. M., and C. N. (1968) 'Students' definition of the objectives of a university education' Australian Journal of Higher Education 3 (2) 111-118
Page 6

KAUFMAN, R. A. (1963) 'The systems approach to programming' in OFIESH, G. D., and MEIERHENRY, W. C. (eds) Trends in programmed instruction (papers from The National Society for Programmed Instruction and Department of Audio-Visual Instruction Conference)
Page 30

KELLER, F. S. (1968) ' "Goodbye, teacher..." ' Journal of Applied Behaviour Analysis 1 (1) 78-89
Pages v, 8, 25

KENNEL, J. H., TEMPIO, C. R., and WILE, M. Z. (1973) 'Self-evaluation by first year medical students in a chemical programme' British Journal of Medical Education 7 (4) 230-238
Page 87

KENSHOLE, G. (1968) 'A teaching experiment in a first-year university course' Physics Education 3 (1) 49-50
Page 52

KING, B. T., and JANIS, I. L. (1956) 'Comparison of the effectiveness of improvised versus non-improvised role-playing in producing opinion changes' Human Relations 9 (2) 177-186
Page 82

KITCHEN, R. D. (1969) 'A study of teaching methods' Australian Journal of Higher Education 3 (3) 218-225
Page 94

KLEIN, J. (1961) Working with groups London, Hutchinson
Page 64

KLEIN, J. (1965) The study of groups London, Routledge and Kegan Paul
Pages 64, 65

KNIGHT, H. R., and SASSENRATH, J. M. (1966) 'Relation of achievement, motivation and test anxiety to performance in programmed instruction' Journal of Educational Psychology 57 (1) 14-17
Page 31

KNOX, J. D. E. (1971) 'The modified essay question' Royal College of General Practitioners
Page 86

KONTIAINEN, S., and COX, R. (1973) 'Attitudes of trainers and trainees to teaching in relation to the objectives of a course for teachers in general practice' London, University Teaching Methods Unit
Page 97

KRUMBOLTZ, J. D., and WEISMAN, R. G. (1962) 'The effect of overt versus covert responding to programmed instruction on immediate and delayed retention' Journal of Educational Psychology 53 (2) 89-92
Page 34

KRUMBOLTZ, J. D. (1964) 'The nature and importance of the required response in programmed instruction' American Journal of Educational Research 1 (4) 203-209
Page 34

LAIDLAW, B., and LAYARD, R. (1974) 'Traditional v. Open University teaching methods: a cost comparison' Higher Education 3 (4) 439-471
Page 14

LANE, M. R. (1974) 'Designing degree courses' Universities Quarterly 28 (2) 219-224

LANGHOLTZ, G., and SEKAY, A. A. (1975) 'Orientations and motivations of freshmen engineers' International Journal of Electrical Engineering Education 12 (3) 255-265
Page 98

LAVACH, J. F., (1973) 'The effect of arousal on short- and long-term memory' Journal of Educational Research 67 (3) 131-133
Page 27

LAWRENCE, G., and ROBINSON, P. (1975) An innovation and its implementation: issues of evaluation London, Tavistock Press

LAYARD, R., and OATEY, M. (1973) 'The cost-effectiveness of the new media in higher education' British Journal of Educational Technology 3 (4) 158-176
Page 14

LAYARD, P. R. G., and VERRY, D. W. (1975) 'Cost functions for university teaching and research' Economic Journal 85 (337) 55-74
Page 14

LE MARNE, A. E. (1972) 'Evaluation of a group controlled audio-visual system of programmed learning' Physics Education 7 (4) 218-224
Page 45

LECKEY, R. C. G. (1972) 'An elementary practical course in electronics for science students' Physics Education 7 (1) 23-26
Page 56

LEE, L. S. and CARTER, G. (1972) 'A sample survey of departments of electrical engineering to determine recent significant changes in laboratory work pattern at first year level' International Journal of Electrical Engineering Education 10 (2) 131-135
Page 75

LEININGER, G. G. (1975) 'Systems engineering — a motivational approach' International Journal of Electrical Engineering Education 12 (3) 197-202
Page 83

LEITH, G. O. M., and BUCKLE, G. F. (1966) Mode of response and non-specific background knowledge Birmingham, National Centre for Research and Documentation of Programmed Learning
Page 33

LEITH, G. O. M. (1969) 'Programmed learning in higher education' in UNWIN, D (ed) Media and methods McGraw Hill
Page 32

LEITH, G. O. M., and McHUGH, G. A. R. (1967) 'The place of theory in learning consecutive conceptual tasks' Educational Review 19 (2) 110-117
Page 23

LEITH, G. O. M., and TROWN, E. A. (1970) 'The influence of personality and task conditions on learning and transfer' Programmed Learning and Educational Technology 7 (3) 181-189
Page 31

LEITH, G. O. M., and WISDOM, B. (1970) 'An investigation of the effects of error making and personality on learning' Programmed Learning and Educational Technology 7 (2) 120-126
Pages 31, 86

LEKAN, H. A. (1970) 'Index to computer assisted instruction' (Stirling Inst.)
Page 53

LEVINE, D., and BENITO, A. J. (1974) 'Impact of clinical training on attitudes of medical students: self-perpetrating barrier to change in the system?' British Journal of Medical Education 8 (1) 13-16
Page 80

LEVINE, F. S. (1974) 'Concepts and models' Education in Chemistry 11 (3) 84-85
Page 28

LEWINSON, D. (1970) 'A self-testing device as an aid to learning' British
Journal of Medical Education 4 (2) 126-129
Page 18

LEWIS, B. N., and PASK, G. (1964) 'The development of communication
skills under adaptively controlled conditions' Programmed Learning
1 (2) 69-88
Page 83

LEWIS, W. P. (1974) 'Observations of problem-solving by engineering
students' The Australian Journal of Education 18 (2) 172-183
Pages 9, 78

LEYTHAM, G. W. H., and JAMES, P. (1973) 'Programmed learning in the
production and presentation of videotaped recordings' Programmed
Learning and Educational Technology 10 (3) 136-143
Page 96

LEYTON, E. (1966) 'The typical lecturer' New Society 7 (193) 12-13
Page 88

LINACRE, E. T. (1973) 'Lessons not lectures' Centre for Advancement of
Teaching Educational Monographs (2) Macquarie University
Page 38

LLOYD, D. H. (1968) 'A concept of improvement of learning response in
the taught lesson' Visual Education (October) 23-25
Page 39

LOEWENTHAL, K., and KOSTREVSKI, B. (1973) 'The effects of training in
written communication or verbal skills' British Journal of
Educational Psychology 43 (1) 82-86
Page 63

LUNT, H. (1973, 1976) (ed) Language and language teaching: current
research in Britain, 1971-2 London, Centre for Information on
Language Teaching and Research
Pages 1, 46-47

LUNT, H. (1974) Survey of research and materials development in voca-
tional uses of English, French and German London, Centre for
Information on Language Teaching and Research
Page 46

MACFARLANE SMITH, I. (1968) 'An experimental study of the effect of
television broadcasts on the G. course in Engineering Science:
1 and 2' The Vocational Aspect of Secondary and Further Education
20 (45) 78-85; 20 (46) 89-100
Page 48

MacKENZIE, A. M. (1974) 'Students in remote areas: an Open University enquiry' Scottish Journal of Adult Education 1 (2) 25-33
Page 61

MacLAINE, A. G. (1965) 'A programme for improving teaching and learning in Australian universities' The Australian University 3 (3) 235-266
Pages 36, 48

MacMANAWAY, L. A. (1968) 'Using lecture scripts' Universities Quarterly 22 (3) 327-336
Page 17

MacMANAWAY, L. A. (1970) 'Teaching methods in higher education — innovation and research' Universities Quarterly 24 (3) 321-329
Pages 25, 92

McCARTHY, M. C. (1968) The employment of highly specialized graduates: a comparative study in the UK and the USA Department of Education and Science Science Policy Studies 3 London, HMSO
Page 6

McCARTHY, W. H. (1970) 'Improving large audience teaching: the "programmed" lecture' British Journal of Medical Education 4 (1) 29-31
Page 24

McCARTHY, W. H., and GONELLA, J. S. (1967) 'The simulated patient management problem' British Journal of Medical Education 1 (5) 348-352
Page 72

McDONALD-ROSS, M. (1972) 'Behavioural objectives and the structure of knowledge' in AUSTWICK, K., and HARRIS, N. D. C. (eds) Aspects of educational technology: Vol. VI London, Pitman
Page 9

McDONALD-ROSS, M., and WALLER, R. (1975) 'Criticism, alternatives and tests: a conceptual framework for improving typography' Programmed Learning and Educational Technology 12 (2) 75-83
Page 60

McDUFFIE, D. E. (1973) 'Learning through practical work' Education in Chemistry 10 (3) 87-88
Page 78

McINTOSH, N. (1974) 'Evaluation of multi-media educational systems: some problems' British Journal of Educational Technology 3 (5) 43-59
Page 96

McKEACHIE, W.J. (1966) 'Research in teaching: the gap between theory and practice' in Improving College Teaching American Council on Education (Washington)
Pages 3, 15, 69

McLEISH, J. (1968a) 'Student retention of lecture material: a methodological study' Cambridge Institute of Education Bulletin 3 (3) 2-11
Page 26

McLEISH, J. (1968b) The lecture method (Cambridge Monographs on Teaching Methods No.1) Cambridge Institute of Education
Pages 26, 39, 93

McLEISH, J. (1970) Students' attitudes and college environments (Cambridge Monographs on Teaching Methods No.3) Cambridge Institute of Education
Pages 90, 93

McNALL, Scott G. (1975) 'Peer teaching: a description and valuation' Teaching Sociology 2 (2) 133-146
Page 66

McVEY, P.J. (1967) Evaluation of four lectures by means of questionnaire (Report No. TR3) University of Surrey Department of Electrical and Control Engineering
Pages 41, 89

MADILL, J.W. (1975) 'The effects of motivational modes and personality types upon academic performance' IEEE Transactions on Education E-18 (3) 144-148
Page 31

MAGER, R.F. (1971) Preparing instructional objectives Palo Alto, California, Fearon Publishers
Page 8

MAIER, N.R.F., and SOLEM, A.R. (1952) 'The contribution of a discussion leader to the quality of group thinking' Human Relations 5 (3) 277-288
Page 65

MALLESON, N. (1967) 'Medical students' study: time and place' British Journal of Medical Education 1 (3) 169-177
Page 86

MALLESON, N., PENFOLD, D., and SAWIRIS, M.Y. (1968) 'Medical students' study: the way they work' British Journal of Medical Education (2) 11-19
Page 57

132

MARINOS, H. G., and LUCAS, A. M. (1971) 'An assessment of audio-tutorial teaching in a plant physiology course' Journal of Biological Education 5 (3) 109-113
Page 97

MARION, P. B. (1974) 'Evaluation of study abroad' ERIC Abstracts 9 (8) (ED 089 634)
Page 81

MARRIS, P. (1965) The experience of higher education London, Routledge and Kegan Paul
Pages 35, 40, 66, 90, 92

MARTIN, D. G., and LEWIS, J. C. (1968) 'Effective laboratory teaching' Bulletin of Mechanical Engineering Education 7 (1) 51-57
Page 78

MEALS, R. A. (1973) 'Teaching clinical judgement — teaching the choice of surgical procedure in the treatment of arthritis of the hip' British Journal of Medical Education 7 (2) 100-102
Page 73

MILES, R. J., and BRAMLEY, Major P. (1974) 'Fatigue and efficiency in learning situations' British Journal of Educational Technology 2 (5) 59-66
Page 27

MILLER, C. M. L., and PARLETT, M (1974) Up to the mark London, Society for Research into Higher Education
Page 95

MILLER, G. (1970) Success, failure and wastage in higher education London, Harrap
Page 21

MILLS, D. G. (1966) 'The use of closed-circuit television in teaching geography and in training teachers of geography' Geography 51 (3) 218-223
Page 49

MINISTRY OF EDUCATION (1956) White paper on technical education (Cmnd 9703) London, HMSO
Page 6

MOORE, D. (1967) 'Group teaching by programmed instruction' Programmed Learning and Educational Technology 4 (1) 37-46
Pages 16, 33, 35

MORRIS, V. A., BLANK, S. S., McKIE, D., and RANKINE, F. C. (1970) 'Motivation, step size, and selected learner variables in relation to performance with programmed instruction' Programmed Learning and Educational Technology 7 (4) 257-267
Page 31

MORRISON, A., and McINTYRE, D. (1967) 'Changes in opinion about education during the first year of teaching' British Journal of Social and Clinical Psychology 6 (3) 161-163
Page 81

MORSTAIN, B.R. (1973) 'Changes in students' educational attitudes: a study of an experimental living-learning programme' Research in Higher Education 1 (2) 141-148
Page 37

MOSCOW, D. (1968) 'The influence of interpersonal variables on the transfer of learning from the T-group to the job situation' Proceedings of the International Congress of Applied Psychology Amsterdam, Swets and Zeitlinger
Page 81

MOSS, J.R. (1973) 'Assessing the learning experience: university students evaluate video-tapes' Programmed Learning and Educational Technology 10 (3) 144-157

MUSGROVE, F. (1969) 'What worries students' Educational Research 12 (1) 56-59
Page 95

NATIONAL UNION OF STUDENTS (1969) Executive report on examinations London, National Union of Students
Pages 40, 76

NAY, M.A., and CROCKER, R.K. (1970) 'Science teaching and the affective attributes of scientists' Science Education 54 (1) 59-67
Page 81

NEALE, D.C. (1967) 'Student ratings of televised classroom demonstrations' Journal of Educational Research 60 (9) 391-393
Page 94

NEWMAN, M.I., WILLIAMS, R.G., and HILLER, J.H. (1974) 'Delay of information feedback in an applied setting: effects of initially learned and unlearned items' Journal of Experimental Education 42 (4) 55-59
Page 24

NIBLETT, B (1976) 'Searching the law by computer' SSRC Newsletter (30) 8
Page 19

NOORDHOF, G.H. (1974) 'The development of self-replay videotape facilities at Brunel University' Programmed Learning and Educational Technology 11 (1) 10-15
Page 51

NUFFIELD FOUNDATION. GROUP FOR RESEARCH AND INNOVATION
IN HIGHER EDUCATION (1974a) 'Interdisciplinarity' in
Newsletter No. 5 7-13
Pages 7, 74

NUFFIELD FOUNDATION. GROUP FOR RESEARCH AND INNOVATION
IN HIGHER EDUCATION (1974b) 'Broader Education' in
Newsletter No. 5 14-19
Page 7

NUFFIELD FOUNDATION. GROUP FOR RESEARCH AND INNOVATION
IN HIGHER EDUCATION (1975) The Drift of Change London,
Nuffield Foundation
Page 7

NUFFIELD FOUNDATION. GROUP FOR RESEARCH AND INNOVATION
IN HIGHER EDUCATION (1976) Units and Modules London,
Nuffield Foundation
Page 7

OLLERENSHAW, Dame K. (1972) 'Manpower planning — the threat of
spur to education' BACIE Journal 26 (2)
Page 6

OOSTHOEK, H., and ACKERS, G. (1973) 'The evaluation of an audio-tape
mediated course: II' British Journal of Educational Technology
1 (4) 54-73
Page 96

ORR, W. G. (1968) 'Retention in comparing programmed and conventional
instructional methods' Journal of Educational Research 62 (1)
11-13
Page 29

OWEN, S. G., HALL, R., ANDERSON, J., and SMART, G. A. (1965)
'A comparison of programmed learning instruction and lectures in
the teaching of electrocardiography' Programmed Learning 2 (1)
2-14
Page 31

PALMER, C. R., and WHITE, G. R. (1974) 'Seminar leader/student and
student/student contacts in university small group teaching'
British Journal of Educational Technology 3 (5) 38-42
Page 64

PALMER, C. R. (1975a) 'Attitudes to learning method in first year
chemistry undergraduates' British Journal of Educational
Technology 6 (2) 47-54
Page 93

PALMER, C. R. (1975b) 'Learning method and preferences in students of chemistry' British Journal of Educational Technology 6 (2) 54-61
Page 93

PALVA, P. (1975) 'Measuring clinical problem solving' British Journal of Medical Education 8 (1) 52-56

PANTALEO, D. C. (1975) 'Video-tapes for laboratory instruction in freshman chemistry' Journal of Chemical Education 52 (2) 112-113
Page 51

PARKER, R. C., and KRISTOL, D. S. (1976) 'Student peer evaluation' Journal of Chemical Education 53 (3) 177-178
Page 66

PARLETT, M., and HAMILTON, D. (1972) 'Evaluation as illumination: a new approach to the study of innovatory programmes' (Occasional Paper 9) University of Edinburgh Centre for Research in the Educational Sciences
Page 9

PASK, G., and SCOTT, B. (1971) Learning strategies and individual competence London, Systems Research Ltd
Page 9

PEEL, E. A. (1968) 'Programmed thinking' in ROBIN, M. J. (ed) Problems and methods in programmed learning (Proceedings of the 1967 Association of Programmed Learning and the National Centre for Programmed Learning Birmingham Conference, 1
Page 31

PERLBERG, A., and RESH, M. (1967) 'Evaluation of the effectiveness of the overhead projector in teaching descriptive geometry and hydrology' Journal of Educational Research 61 (1) 14-18
Page 43

PERROTT, E., APPLEBEE, A. N., WATSON, E., and HEAP, B. (1975a) 'A self-instructional microteaching course on effective questioning' Peterborough, Guild of Sound and Vision 3 vols: teachers' handbook, co-ordinators' guide, and evaluation manual; and 5 videotape or film programmes
Page 49

PERROTT, E., APPLEBEE, A. N., WATSON, E., and HEAP, B. (1975b) 'Changes in teaching behaviour after completing a self-instructional microteaching course' Programmed Learning and Educational Technology 12 (6) 348-362
Page 49

PERROTT, E., APPLEBEE, A. N., WATSON, E., and HEAP, B. (1975c) (in press) 'An investigation into teachers' reactions to a self-instructional micro-teaching course'
Page 49

PERROTT, E., and DUTHIE, J.H. (1969) 'University television in action micro-teaching' University Television Newsletter 7
Page 50

PIAGET, J. (1972) 'The epistemology of interdisciplinary relationships' in Interdisciplinarity — problems of teaching and research in universities Paris, Centre for Educational Research and Development, OECD
Page 7

PICKFORD, M. (1975) 'University inputs, outputs and educational technology' British Journal of Educational Technology 6 (2) 61-70
Page 14

PIKAS, A. (1969) 'Comparisons between traditional and programmed learning as a function of passive performance and active application, and time till application' Programmed Learning and Educational Technology 6 (1) 20-25
Page 29

PIPER, D.W. (1967) 'Strategies in course planning' Design Education (2) 16-18
Page 10

POOLE, Millicent M. (1971) 'Social class differences in code elaboration: a study of oral communication at the tertiary level' The Australian Journal of Education 15 152-160
Page 61

POPPLETON, P.K., and AUSTWICK, K. (1964) 'A comparison of programmed learning and note-taking at two age levels' British Journal of Educational Psychology 34 (1) 43-50
Page 34

POSTLETHWAIT, S.N., NOVAK, J., and MURRAY, H. (1964) An integrated experience approach to learning Minneapolis, Burgess Publishing
Pages v, 8

POULTON, E.C. (1961) 'British courses for adults on effective reading' British Journal of Educational Psychology 31 (II) 128-137
Page 57

POWER, T.V. (1972) 'In search of objectives for introductory courses in English law' Vocational Aspects of Education 24 (59) 123-131
Page 11

PREECE, D.A., and FLOOD PAGE, C. (1974) 'Sandwich course undergraduates and industrial experience' Vocational Aspects of Education 26 (65) 95-104
Page 81

PRESTON, B. (1975) 'Attendance beats track record in the degree stakes' Times Higher Education Supplement 3 Jan 1975
Page 38

PROSSER, A. P. (1967) 'Oral reports on laboratory work' in Teaching for
Efficient Learning (report of a conference held at the University of
London Institute of Education) London, University Teaching Methods
Research Unit
Page 62

RASHEED, R. N. (1967) 'The relationship between factors of personality
and academic achievement in a programmed learning situation among
college students' Dissertation Abstracts International 31 (4-A) 1646
Page 31

READ, F. (1969) 'New techniques for the teaching of practical physics'
Physics Education 4 77-81
Page 78

REID-SMITH, E. R. (1969) 'The measurement of level of student satisfaction
by means of a course assessment questionnaire' Research in
Librarianship 10 (2) 100-107
Page 98

REPIN, V., and ORLOV, R. S. (1967) 'The use of sleep and relaxation in
the study of foreign languages' Australian Journal of Psychology
19 (3) 203-207
Page 27

RICHARDSON, I. M., and HOWIE, J. G. R. (1972) 'A study of trainee general
practitioners' British Journal of Medical Education 6 (1) 29-31
Page 73

ROBERTSON, R. G. (1969) 'Teaching engineering by television' Chartered
Mechanical Engineer 16 January 15-18
Page 51

ROBINSON, F. P. (1961) Effective study Harper and Row
Page 61

ROSS, D. (1972-6) Courses in legal practice Melbourne, Leo Cussen
Institute for Continuing Legal Education
Pages 9, 70, 72

ROWNTREE, D. (1973) What is educational technology? (Monograph No. 1)
Milton Keynes, The Open University Institute of Educational Technology
Page 8

ROYAL COLLEGE OF GENERAL PRACTITIONERS (1969) 'Report of the
Vocational Training Sub-Committee: educational needs of the future
general practitioner' Journal of the Royal College of General
Practitioners 18 (89) 358-360
Pages 12, 86

ROYAL COMMISSION ON MEDICAL EDUCATION 1965-66 (1969) The Todd
Report London, HMSO
Pages 85, 90, 91

138

SAUNDERS, M. et al (1969) Report of the Commission on Teaching in Higher Education London, National Union of Students
Pages 21, 36, 90, 91, 92

SAVAGE, R. D. (1972) 'An exploratory study of individual characteristics associated with attainment in medical school' British Journal of Medical Education 6 (1) 68-77

SAVAGE, R. D. (1974) 'Personality and achievement in higher education professional training' Educational Review 27 (1) 3-15

SAYER, S., and HARDING, A. G. (1974) 'Time to look beyond technology to better use of human resources Times Higher Education Supplement 20 December 1974
Page 13

SCHONELL, F.J. et al (1961a) 'Australian university experiment: problem and promise' Australian Journal of Science 24 (1) 19-20
Page 87

SCHONELL, F.J. et al (1961b) University teaching in Queensland (Report of conferences for demonstrators and lecturers) Brisbane, University of Queensland Press
Page 87

SCHONELL, F.J., ROE, E., and MIDDLETON, I. G. (1962) Promise and performance Brisbane, University of Queensland Press
Pages 36, 90

SCLARE, A. B., and THOMPSON, G. O. B. (1968) 'The use of closed-circuit television in teaching psychiatry to medical students' British Journal of Medical Education 2 (3) 226-228
Page 48

SCOTT, N. C., DONNELLY, M. B., GALLAGHER, R., and HESS, J. W. (1973) 'Interaction analysis as a method of assessing skill in relating to patients: studies on validity' British Journal of Medical Education (7) 174-178
Page 63

SECURRO, S., and WALLS, R. T. (1975) 'Strategies for increasing self-initiated interaction' Journal of Educational Research 68 (8) 283-285
Page 64

SENTER, R.J. et al (1966) An experimental comparison of an intrinsically programmed text and a narrative text (Final Report No. AMRL-TR-65-227) Ohio, Aero-Space Medical Research Laboratories, Wright Patterson AFB
Page 30

SEYMOUR, W. D. (1937) 'An experiment showing the superiority of a light-coloured "blackboard" ' British Journal of Educational Psychology 7 (3) 259-268
Page 43

SEYMOUR, W. D. (1966) Industrial skills London, Pitman
Pages 54, 55

SHADBOLT, D. R., and LEITH, G. O. M. (1967) 'Mode of learning and personality' (mimeo) University of Birmingham National Centre for Programmed Learning
Page 31

SHELDRAKE, P. (1974) 'Behavioural science: medical students' expectations and reactions' British Journal of Medical Education 8 (1) 31-48
Page 97

SHERMAN, B., and BLACKBURN, R. T. (1974) ERIC Abstracts 9 (8) (ED 089 620)
Page 88

SHOUKSMITH, G. (1969) 'Experimental psychology in large introductory classes' Bulletin of the British Psychological Society 22 (77) 293-296
Page 79

SIEBRING, B. R., and SCHAFF, M. E. (1974) 'A survey of the literature concerning student evaluation of teaching' Journal of Chemical Education 51 (3) 150
Page 42

SIME, M., and BOYCE, G. (1969) 'Overt responses, knowledge and results of learning' Programmed Learning and Educational Technology 6 (1) 12-19
Page 33

SIMPSON, R. H. (1965) 'The use of self-evaluation procedures by lecturers in educational psychology' Educational Review 18 (1) 25-33
Page 42

SMITH, A. D., and JEPSON, J. B. (1972) '"Variation of the information game" for use in a preclinical biochemistry course' The Lancet 1972 2 Sept 16 585-586
Page 63

SMITH, G. (1974) 'Is closed circuit television a worthwhile teaching aid?' British Journal of Medical Education (8) 218-220
Page 48

SMITH, G., and WYLLIE, J. H. (1965) 'Use of closed-circuit television in teaching surgery to medical students' British Medical Journal (2) 99-101
Page 48

SMITH, G., WYLLIE, J. H., FORTE, A. V., and CARADIS, D. T. (1966)
'Further studies of the use of closed-circuit television in teaching
surgery to undergraduate students' British Journal of Medical
Education (1) 40-42
Page 48

SMITH, P. B. (1964) 'Attitude changes associated with training in human
relations' British Journal of Social and Clinical Psychology 2 (2)
104-112
Page 80

SMITH, P. B., and POLLACK, H. B. (1968) 'The participant's learning style
as a correlate of T-group learning' Proceedings of the International
Conference of Applied Psychology Amsterdam, Swets and Zeitlinger
Page 81

SMITH, P. B. (1969a) Improving skills in working with people: the T-group
(Training Information Paper 4) London, HMSO
Page 80

SMITH, P. B. (1969b) 'T-group climate, trainer style and some tests of
learning' in MILES, M. B., and HJELHOLT, G. (eds) Group
Development National Training Laboratories
Pages 80, 91

SMITH, R. N. (1971) 'Assessment of a programmed instructional text in
clinical pharmacology' British Journal of Medical Education (5)
325-327
Page 96

SMITHERS, A. C. (1970a) 'Some factors in lecturing' Educational Review
22 (2) 141-150
Page 42

SMITHERS, A. C. (1970b) 'What do students expect of lectures?'
Universities Quarterly 3 Summer 330-336
Page 42

SMITHERS, A. C. (1976) The sandwich course: an integrated experience?
National Foundation for Educational Research
Pages 20, 95

SNADDEN, R. B., and RUNQUIST, O. (1975) 'Simulated experiments'
Education in Chemistry 12 (3) 75-77
Page 73

SOLOFF, Sheila (1973) 'Effect of non-content factors on the grading of essays'
Graduate Research in Education and Related Disciplines 6 Spring 44-54
Page 62

SPECIAL CORRESPONDENT (1966a) 'Necropsy demonstrations relayed by
television' British Medical Journal (1) 478
Page 50

SPECIAL CORRESPONDENT (1966b) 'Closed-circuit television between
medical schools' British Medical Journal 1 1476-1477
Page 50

SPROTT, W.J.H. (1958) Human groups Harmondsworth, Penguin
Page 64

STAHL, S.M., HENNES, J.D., and FLEISCHLI, G. (1975) 'Progress on
self-learning in biostatics' Journal of Medical Education (50)
294-296
Page 60

STANSFIELD, J.M. (1971) 'From a postgraduate centre: a multiple choice
examination test on postgraduate lectures' British Journal of
Medical Education 5 (4) 307-308
Page 97

STANTON, H.E. (1975) 'Music and test anxiety: further evidence for an
interaction' British Journal of Educational Psychology 45 (1) 80-82
Page 27

STARTUP, R., and GRUNEBERG, M.M. (1976) 'The rewards of research'
New Universities Quarterly 30 (2) 225-238
Page 88

STAVERT, G.S. (1969) 'Programmed learning in action' BACIE Journal
23 (1) 16-20
Page 34

STAVERT, G.S., and WINGATE, T.H. (1966) 'Nelson's Navy needed none
but... ! ' Tutor Age (17) 2-7
Pages 16, 34

STEEDMAN, W. (1974) 'The chemical literature — an undergraduate course'
Education in Chemistry 11 (3) 93
Page 61

STEINBERG, H., and LEWIS, H.E. (1951) 'An experiment on the teaching
value of a scientific film British Medical Journal (2) 465-471
Page 51

STEWART-TULL, D.E.S. (1970) 'The setting and marking of microbiology
examinations' Journal of Biological Education 4 (1) 25-42
Page 85

STONES, E. (1966) 'The effects of different conditions of working on student
performance and attitudes' Programmed Learning 3 (3) 135-145
Page 33

STONES, E. (1967) 'Strategies and tactics in programmed instruction' in
TOBIN, M.J. (ed) Problems and methods in programmed learning
(proceedings of the Association of Programmed Learning and National
Centre for Programmed Learning Birmingham Conference) 62
Page 30

STONES, E. (1969) 'Students' attitudes to the size of teaching groups' Educational Review 21 (2) 98-108
Pages 90, 92

STRETTON, T. B., HALL, R., and OWEN, S. G. (1967) 'Programmed learning in medical education: comparison of teaching machine and programmed textbook' British Journal of Medical Education 1 (3) 165-168
Page 34

STUDENTS' SOCIETY COMMITTEE OF ROYAL DENTAL HOSPITAL SCHOOL OF DENTAL SURGERY (1966) 'Report on opinion poll on the lecture courses' Supplement to Extract 33 (I)
Pages 36, 39, 90

STUEBNER, E. A., and JOHNSON, R. P. (1969) 'A hospital clerkship programme for dental students: an exploratory study' Journal of Dental Education 33 (2) 224-229
Page 20

SULLIVAN, R. M. (1974) 'Psychology in teaching' Canadian Journal of Behavioural Science 6 (1) 1-28
Pages 24, 28, 96

COMMITTEE ON MANPOWER RESOURCES FOR SCIENCE AND TECHNOLOGY (1968) Swann Report: the flow into employment of scientists, engineers and technologists London, HMSO (CMND. 3760)
Page 6

TANSEY, P. J. (1969) 'Simulation and teacher education' Education for Teaching 79 Summer 63-68
Page 73

TAPLIN, G. (1969) 'The Cosford Cube: a simplified form of student feed-back' Industrial Training International 4 (5) 218-219
Page 24

TAYLOR, J. L., and MADDISON, R. (1968) 'A land use gaming simulation: the design of a model for the study of urban phenomena' Urban Affairs Quarterly 3 (4) June
Page 72

TAYLOR, J. L., and CARTER, K. R. (1967) 'Instructional simulation or urban development: a preliminary report' Town Planning Institute Journal 53 (10) 443-447
Page 72

TAYLOR, R. G., and HANSON, G. R. (1969) 'Pre-college mathematics workshop and freshman achievement' Journal of Educational Research 64 (3) 157-160
Page 20

TEATHER, D. C. B. (1968) 'Programmed learning in biology' Journal of
Biological Education 2 (3) 119-135
Page 17

TEATHER, D. C. B. (1974) 'Learning from film: a significant difference
between the effectiveness of different projection methods'
Programmed Learning and Educational Technology 11 (6) 328-334
Page 51

TEATHER, D. C. B., and MARCHANT, H. (1974) 'Learning from film with
special reference to the effects of cueing, questioning, and knowledge
of results' Programmed Learning and Educational Technology 11 (6)
328-334
Page 26

THODAY, D. (1957) 'How undergraduates work' Universities Quarterly
11 (2) 172-181
Page 20

THORNDIKE, E. L. (1913) The psychology of learning New York,
Columbia University Teachers College
Page 66

TOBIN, M. J. (1968) 'Technical education and industrial training'
Educational Technology 10 (11) 442-444
Pages 30, 31, 34

TRENAMAN, T. M. (1967) Communication and comprehension London,
Longmans
Pages 39, 49

TRENT, J. W., and COHEN, A. M. (1973) 'Research on teaching in higher
education' in TRAVERS, R. M. W. (ed) Second handbook of research
on teaching American Educational Research Association (Rand
McNally)
Page 3

TROPP, A. (1969) 'Objectives from the point of view of a sociologist' in
UTMU (ed) Conference on objectives in higher education London,
University Teaching Methods Unit
Page 5

TROWN, A. (1970) 'Some evidence on the interaction of teaching strategy
and personality' British Journal of Educational Psychology 40 (2)
209-211
Page 86

TUBBS, M. R. (1968) 'Seminars in experimental physics' Physics Education
3 (4) 189-192
Pages 15, 16

TUCKMAN, J., and LORGE, I (1962) 'Individual ability as a determinant
of group superiority' Human Relations 15 (1) 45-57
Page 65

UNIVERSITY OF BREMEN (1976) Proceedings of the International
Conference on Project Orientation   University of Bremen
Page 8

UNIVERSITY GRANTS COMMITTEE (1964) Report of the Committee on
University Teaching Methods (Hale Committee)   London, HMSO
Pages 5, 35, 38, 90

UNIVERSITY GRANTS COMMITTEE, DEPARTMENT OF EDUCATION AND
SCIENCE, and SCOTTISH EDUCATION DEPARTMENT (1965)
Report of the Committee on Audio-Visual Aids in Higher Scientific
Education (Brynmer Jones Committee)   London, HMSO·
Pages 5, 45

UNIVERSITY OF LEEDS INSTITUTE OF EDUCATION (1973) The objectives
of teacher education   Slough, National Foundation for Educational
Research
Page 12

UNIVERSITY TEACHING METHODS RESEARCH UNIT (1968) Innovations
and experiments in university teaching methods (report of the third
conference organized by the Unit) London, UTMU
Page 67

UREN, O. (1968) The use of texts in language skill development: some
problems (report of the third conference organized by the Unit)
London, University Teaching Methods Research Unit
Page 67

VALVERDI, H. H., and MORGAN, R. L. (1970) 'Influence on student achieve-
ment of redundancy in self-instructional materials Programmed
Learning and Educational Technology 7 (3) 194-199
Page 16

VAN DER KLAUW, C. F., and PLOMP, T. T. (1974) 'Individualised study
system in theory and practice' Higher Education 3 (2) 213-230
Page 96

VAN ZOOST, B. L., and JACKSON, B. T. (1974) 'Effects of self-monitoring
and self-administered reinforcement on study behaviours' Journal of
Educational Research 67 January 216-218
Page 56

VARAGUNAM, T. (1971) 'Student awareness of behavioural objectives: the
effect of learning' British Journal of Medical Education 5 (2)
213-216
Page 8

VERNON, M. D. (1953) 'Perception and understanding of instructional television programmes' British Journal of Psychology 44 (2) 116-126
Page 49

VERNON, P. E. (1946) 'An experiment on the value of the film and film-strip in the instruction of adults' British Journal of Educational Psychology 16 (3) 149-162
Page 51

WALLIS, D., DUNCAN, K. D., and KNIGHT, M. A. G. (1966) 'The Halton experiment and the Melksham experiment' in Programmed Instruction in the British Armed Forces London, HMSO
Page 16

WALTON, H. J., and DREWERY, J. (1964) 'Teaching psychiatry to under-graduate medical students' Journal of Medical Education 29 (6) 545-552
Page 11

WALTON, H. J., and DREWERY, J. (1966) 'Psychiatrists as teachers in medical schools' British Journal of Psychiatry 112 839-846
Page 11

WALTON, H. J., and DREWERY, J. (1967) 'The objective examination in the evaluation of medical students' British Journal of Medical Education 1 (4) 255-264
Page 85

WASON, P. C. (1970) 'On writing scientific papers' Physics Bulletin 21 407-408
Page 62

WASON, P. C. (1973) 'Are there rules for writing English?' (ICL Lectures on Technical Communication) University of Wales Institute of Science and Technology
Page 62

WASON, P. C. (1974) 'Notes on the supervision of PhDs' Bulletin of the British Psychological Society 27 (94) 25-9
Page 62

WENDLANDT, W. W., GEANANGEL, R. A., and BARRY, D. (1975) 'A tape-slide freshman chemistry course for non-science majors' Journal of Chemical Education 52 (2) 110-111
Page 45

WHALLEY, P. C., and FLEMING, R. W. (1975) 'An experiment with a simple recorder of reading behaviour' Programmed Learning and Educational Technology 12 (2) 120-124
Page 44

WHITELAND, J. W. R. (1966) 'The selection of research students' Universities Quarterly 21 (1) 44-47
Page 75

WILBY, P. (1976) 'A rare generosity of spirit' Times Higher Education Supplement 13 February 1976
Page 7

WILCOX, B. (1974) 'The teaching of serial tasks using chaining strategies' British Journal of Educational Psychology 44 (2) 175-183
Page 55

WILLIAMS, J. P. (1963) 'Comparison of several modes in a review programme' Journal of Educational Psychology 54 253-260
Page 34

WILLIS, F., DOBLE, G., SANKARAYA, U., and SMITHERS, A. G. (1977) Residence abroad and the student of modern languages (University of Bradford, in preparation)
Page 47

WILSON, J. D. (1971) 'Predicting levels of first year university performance' British Journal of Educational Psychology 41 (2) 167-170
Page 86

WILSON, J. F. (1966) 'A survey of legal education in the UK' The Journal of the Society of Public Teachers of Law 9 (1) 1-44
Page 38

de WINTER HEBRON, C. C. (1974) 'Self instruction versus lecturer instruction using tape-slide in a library induction programme' Bulletin of Educational Research 7 12-15 (SRHE Abstracts 8 (3) 187)
Page 44

WITTERS, D. R., and KENT, G. W. (1972) 'Teaching without lecturing: evidence in the case of individualised instruction' The Psychological Record (22) 169-175
Pages 24, 96

WOMERSLEY, J., STENHOUSE, G., and DUNN, W. R. (1974) 'Use of a response system' British Journal of Medical Education 5 (3) 192-196
Page 38

WOOD, C. C., and HEDLEY, R. L. (1968) 'Student reaction to VTR in simulated classroom conditions' Canadian Educational Research Digest 8 (1) 46-59
Pages 49, 50

WOOD, D. N. (1969) 'Library education for scientists and engineers' Bulletin of Mechanical Engineering Education 8 (1) 1-9
Page 61

WOOD, K., LINSKY, A. S., and STRAUSS, M. A. (1975) 'Class size and student evaluation of faculty' Journal of Higher Education 45 (7) 524-534

WOODFORD, F. P. (1972) 'Experiences in teaching scientific writing in the
    USA' Journal of Biological Education 6 (1) 9-12
    Page 62

WOODFORD, G. A. (1969) 'Teacher influence in a college of education'
    Educational Research 11 (2) 148-152
    Page 93

WOODING, E. R. (1968) 'Third-year laboratory projects in physics' in
    UTMU (ed) Innovations and Experiments in University Teaching
    Methods 75-80   London, University Teaching Methods Research Unit.
    Page 76

WOODS, C. S., and NORTHCOTT, P. H. (1970) An audio-visual innovation in
    undergraduate teaching: a progress report   Australian Geography
    Teachers Association
    Page 46

WOOLFENDEN, P. J. (1969) 'Objectives in medical education' in UTMU
    (ed) Objectives in higher education   London, University Teaching
    Methods Unit
    Page 9

WRAGG, E. C. (1970) 'Interaction analysis as a feedback system for student
    teachers' Education for Teaching 81 Spring 38-47
    Page 89

WRIGHT, E. A. (1968) 'A research project for clinical medical students'
    in Innovations and experiments in university teaching methods
    see UNIVERSITY TEACHING METHODS UNIT above
    Pages 58, 76, 78

WRIGHT, P. (1967) 'The use of questions in programmed learning'
    Programmed Learning and Educational Technology 4 (2) 103-107
    Page 34

WRIGHT, P. (1968) 'Reading to learn' Chemistry in Britain 4 (10) 445-450
    Page 58

WYATT, H. V. (1975) 'An introductory microbiology course based on the
    Clothier Report' Journal of Biological Education 9 (1) 21-25
    Page 96

ZILLMAN, D., and CANTOR, J. R. (1973) 'Induction of curiosity in
    rhetorical questions and its effect on the learning of factual materials'
    British Journal of Educational Psychology 43 (2) 172-180
    Page 37

148

INDEX